The Economic Policy of Online Media

This book explores the distortion of communication online, centered around the theory that the economic policy model of online media is primarily based on the systematic manufacture of dissent.

Following the media criticism tradition of Habermas and Chomsky, among others, the book shows how anger can motivate news consumption as the principle of divide-and-rule in the online media of the 21st century is systematically applied. The author posits that media addiction increases interest, therefore deliberate distortion of facts and the manufacture of dissent provide the media with a larger audience and this becomes the business model.

This insightful volume will interest researchers, scholars, and students of media economics, political economy of media, digital media, propaganda, mass communication, and media literacy.

Peter Ayolov is Assistant Professor in the Faculty of Journalism and Mass Communication at Sofia University 'St. Kliment Ohridski', Bulgaria.

Routledge Studies in Media, Communication, and Politics

9. Hate Speech and Polarisation in Participatory Society
   Edited by Marta Pérez-Escolar, José Manuel Noguera-Vivo

10. White Supremacy and the American Media
    Edited By Sarah D. Nilsen, Sarah E. Turner

11. Tweeting Brexit
    Social Media and the Aftermath of the EU Referendum
    Maja Šimunjak

12. Knowledge Resistance in High-Choice Information Environments
    Edited By Jesper Strömbäck, Åsa Wikforss, Kathrin Glüer, Torun Lindholm, Henrik Oscarsson

13. A Media Framing Approach to Securitization
    Storytelling in Conflict, Crisis, and Threat
    Fred Vultee

14. Gender Violence, Social Media, and Online Environments
    When the Virtual Becomes Real
    Lisa M. Cuklanz

15. Right-Wing Media's Neurocognitive and Societal Effects
    Rodolfo Levya

16. The Economic Policy of Online Media
    Manufacture of Dissent
    Peter Ayolov

For more information about this series, please visit: www.routledge.com/Routledge-Studies-in-Media-Communication-and-Politics/book-series/RSMCP

The Economic Policy of Online Media
Manufacture of Dissent

Peter Ayolov

LONDON AND NEW YORK

First published 2023
by Routledge
4 Park Square, Milton Park, Abingdon, Oxon OX14 4RN

and by Routledge
605 Third Avenue, New York, NY 10158

Routledge is an imprint of the Taylor & Francis Group, an informa business

© 2023 Peter Ayolov

The right of Peter Ayolov to be identified as author of this work has been asserted in accordance with sections 77 and 78 of the Copyright, Designs and Patents Act 1988.

All rights reserved. No part of this book may be reprinted or reproduced or utilised in any form or by any electronic, mechanical, or other means, now known or hereafter invented, including photocopying and recording, or in any information storage or retrieval system, without permission in writing from the publishers.

Trademark notice: Product or corporate names may be trademarks or registered trademarks, and are used only for identification and explanation without intent to infringe.

British Library Cataloguing-in-Publication Data
A catalogue record for this book is available from the British Library

ISBN: 978-1-032-45946-2 (hbk)
ISBN: 978-1-032-46136-6 (pbk)
ISBN: 978-1-003-38020-7 (ebk)

DOI: 10.4324/9781003380207

Typeset in Sabon
by Apex CoVantage, LLC

Contents

Introduction: the Civil Cold War online   1

1   Changing the paradigm of mass communication   7

    1.1. *The need for a new paradigm* 7
    1.2. *The rise of dissent in the network society* 14
    1.3. *The 'New World Information Order' dystopia* 24
    1.4. *Dysfunctions in the propaganda model* 30

2   Dissent and the theory of mass communication   38

    2.1. *'Manufacture of consent'—Walter Lippmann* 38
    2.2. *'Democratic propaganda'—Edward Bernays* 43
    2.3. *'The spiral of silence'—Elizabeth Noelle-Neumann* 47
    2.4. *'The propaganda model'—Noam Chomsky and Edward Herman* 51
    2.5. *'The end of history'—Francis Fukuyama* 56
    2.6. *'Agenda setting'—Maxwell McCombs* 61
    2.7. *'Pseudo news'—Niklas Luhmann* 63
    2.8. *'Distorted communication'—Jürgen Habermas* 66

3   Digital media as a risk to democracy   75

    3.1. *Digital capitalism and decorative democracy* 75
    3.2. *Trust and dissent in democracy* 79
    3.3. *Dissidents' dissent and cognitive infiltration* 86

4   Mass media as dissent manufacture   94

    4.1. *The Bulgarian connection in the attack on the pope* 94
    4.2. *The effect of the 'lying press' (Lügenpresse)* 97
    4.3. *Doublespeak and conflict propaganda* 101
    4.4. *The language of Russophilia/Russophobia* 103

Conclusion: the dissent of the governed 112

1. *Media hostility index 112*
2. *Angry citizens of the internet 114*
3. *Second-degree cybernetics and Kayfabe 117*
4. *Planned obsolescence of communication 120*

Index 128

Introduction
The Civil Cold War online

Peter Ayolov

> 'Qohen Leth:—Why would you want to prove that all is for nothing?
> Management:—I never said all is for nothing. I'm a businessman, Mr. Leth, nothing is for nothing. Ex inordinateo veni pecunia.
> Qohen Leth:—What?
> Management:—There's money in ordering disorder.
> Chaos pays, Mr. Leth!'
>
> The Zero Theorem (2013)

Manufacture (n.)

1560s, 'something made by hand', from French manufacture (16c.), from Medieval Latin *manufactura 'a making by hand' *manufacture* (v.) 1680s, 'convert material to a form suitable for use', Meaning 'to make or fabricate', especially in considerable quantities or numbers, as by the aid of many hands or machinery is by 1755. Figurative sense of 'produce artificially, invent fictitiously, get up by contrivance or effort' is from 1762.

Dissent (v.)

1580s, 'difference of opinion with regard to religious doctrine or worship', from the verb. From 1650s as 'the act of dissenting, refusal to be bound by what is contrary to one's own judgment' (the opposite of consent). From 1660s as 'a declaration of disagreement.' By 1772 in the specific sense of 'refusal to conform to an established church.'

At the beginning of the 21st century, after the 2010 Arab Spring, the 2011 Syrian Civil War, and the 2013 conflict in Ukraine, the agenda of global media has once again included the topic of conflict propaganda. The issue became popular in the early 20th century and propaganda campaigns from the First and Second World Wars. After massive media campaigns of black propaganda at the beginning of both centuries, violent clashes, civil wars, military coups, and street revolutions followed. In many cases, they lead to the abolition of democracy and the beginning of authoritarian regimes. These propaganda wars in the mass media in the early 20th and 21st centuries are a systematic model for the manufacture of dissent that deflates trust in society and gives birth to solid anti-statist trends. Conflict propaganda's ancient military and political strategies are turned into a communication strategy. Dissent became so crucial for liberal democracies as consent for all governments. In the new century, the arena for these wars of ideas is the virtual space of the Internet. They are no longer just clashes between different national ideologies and interests. Propaganda wars are still being fought in the public sphere of nation-states, but the ideologies and interests are global and supranational. Western democracies became an arena for international economic battles masked as ideological wars. The principal victim of this hybrid war is the unity of society and the trust in state government. With the help of the Internet and social media, traditional societies in democracies are increasingly divided into different groups in constant dissent. The old divide-and-rule model and the idea of the failed state are revived in cyberspace. The Internet as a 'fifth estate' controls the growing masses but divides them into hostile groups. These new virtual nations are global, and their members are citizens of foreign countries but are united by shared beliefs and lifestyles. In many cases, this new pseudo-ideology points to a shared universal enemy. Thus, the Cold War between states was transformed into a propaganda civil war, and the truth became only the opinion of the interested party. This time the goal is not in the clash between nations but the division of society into separate warring ideological factions. Individuals find identity in a climate of conflict and hatred against their enemies. This moral dualism has led to the return of conflict propaganda from the early 20th century. This time, however, in the new conditions of the Internet. Thus, polarisation, division, and dissent between the groups in the online media audience become a significant effect of mass communication. This book offers the hypothesis that in the 21st century, the digital mass media industry works as a manufacturer of dissent even when claiming the opposite.

Propaganda is a mass communication strategy for forming public opinion favoring specific interests. The social role of democratic propaganda is to create consent through open dialogue in the mass media. Thus, the consent of the governed legitimises power in a democratic state. In contrast, conflict propaganda manufactures dissent between the various groups in society. It creates an image of a universal enemy by instilling anger and fear. In democracies, the entry of the Internet and the lack of censorship have reduced the protective role of national propaganda. On the other hand, corporate and foreign propaganda are booming. It is no longer possible to form independent public opinion in the majority population. Instead, there is a strategic disagreement and divide on basic principles. The newly created groups are set against each other by the divide-and-rule online model. Public opinion techniques are changing on the Internet, as are the communities on social networks. The pattern of disagreement on the Internet is beginning to create tensions within the democratic states. Strong anti-democratic trends are emerging, similar to the processes of the early 20th century. There are parallel anti-statist ideologies in favor of multinational organisations. The effects of this are general distrust, not only of statehood and institutions but also between people. The neoliberal idea that Big Society can replace national societies by integrating the free market with a theory of social solidarity is just a theory. The policies toward a small government also lead to a small society that is not capable or willing to govern itself. The core of democratic ideology is the continuous movement toward deliberation and direct democracy instead of new ways of representation. In a representative democracy, mass media plays a primary role in forming opinions. This process is more sophisticated on the Internet, and instead, public opinion social media is forming human identities and communities. The result is just a façade democracy because deliberation needs education, trust, and participation. Instead of creating a New World Information Order of direct democracy, the Internet materialised the Huxleyan–Orwellian nightmare of surveillance neo-feudalism.

To better understand these processes in the 21st century, a revision of democratic theories is needed, especially regarding public communication and the role of propaganda. The state, business, and media intervention in the formation of public opinion are at the heart of the democratic theory of the 20th century. These processes are related to mass communication technologies and manipulation techniques after the First World War. The media as a fourth estate is at the heart of government in the age of mass communication. It is public opinion, the consent of the governed, and the will of the people that legitimises any power. The question of how public opinion is formed in modern democracy is subject to debate by the time of John Dewey and Walter Lippmann. John Dewey believes that society is a single and active agent in the accessible and information-saturated public communication of liberal democracies. It can only form a reasonable and educated public opinion, under which the state should be guided. Sociologists and the media are only to register public opinion. They can enhance its effect by spreading it. On the other hand, Walter Lippmann believes there should be a special class of competent people. With the help of mass media, an educated elite must form this opinion that guarantees the unity and consent of society. Lippmann calls it the 'manufacture of consent.' He believes that there will be dissent and chaos in society without outside interference. The dilemma of democracy is if bias-free communication tends toward order or chaos. Dewey or Lippman? More democracy and education or more guidance and control? Despite the enormous amount of literature and research, there is no winner in this debate. There is no unequivocal view on the mechanism of public opinion in the development of democracy. The lack of clarity on who and how should shape public opinion creates constant crises of trust in democratic societies. The crisis of democracy, which has occurred in parallel with the entry of the Internet media, is associated with distrust of traditional media models of monopoly information control. Freedom of expression and easy access to information on the Internet completely change the old communication paradigm. The 'manufacture of consent' model in nation-states no longer works, leading to the accumulation of tension and disagreement. This crisis calls for a new reading of the classic media theories in search of a change in democratic ideology. The only way for the ideology to change is through the emergence of new elites. The ruling ideas usually are the ideas of the ruling classes, and as the digital business giants of the Internet are growing, the term digital capitalism is in use. As a new communication model is sought, dissent is becoming more and more prevalent in online media and human societies.

In 1970, Jürgen Habermas introduced the concept of 'systematically distorted communication' about the primary problems of the model of domination and power in the system of mass communication. The hypothesis of the 'manufacture of dissent' model in online media is part of this tradition. This type of communication distortion does not aim at consent and connections between people, but division, conflict, and disagreement. Habermas aims to detect distorted communication in the mass media and reconstruct conditions for unity and understanding. Communication must seek mutual understanding, shared knowledge, trust, and coherence, which provoke an agreement that ends in the intersubjective joint. For Habermas, consent is based on jointly recognised four relevant claims for validity: understandability, truth, truthfulness, and correctness. Once this consensus is shaken and at least one of the claims for validity is invalid, the communicative action cannot be continued. In his 1979 essay 'What is universal pragmatics?'[1] Habermas looks for normative conditions for possible understanding, an aspiration to universal grammar, and the general validity of speech. It requires a negative approach to seeking violations based on the validity of speech. Public speech may be generally distorted and invalid, preventing agreement and understanding. The communicative action cannot be continued, and no agreement can be reached. Once the speech is not valid, the communication is distorted into pseudo-communication. It begins to produce disagreement. In many cases, the problem of mass communication is the damaged speech used by traditional mass media and institutions in the name of their interests. This doublespeak is an instrument of power and a means of social control. It manufactures consent, but only within the group. On the other hand, it creates tension and hostility against other groups in society. Dissent is an old problem for democratic societies, but with the advent of the Internet media, the war of ideas is spreading within the state. The problem is that without censorship and media regulation, controlling natural disagreement in democracy is difficult. New media and social networks on the Internet lead to a division of society and gain enormous political, cultural, and social power. The divide-and-rule model works as well on the Internet as in the past, and the signs of the new paradigm of communication are contained in the media theories of the 20th century. The first task is to analyze known texts and theories given the new digital media conditions. The path to understanding future development trends is

Introduction 5

a profound analysis and a new understanding of familiar research. Some of the authors whose ideas are analyzed in connection with the manufacture of the dissent model are Walter Lippmann, Edward Bernays, Marshall McLuhan, Edward S. Herman, Noam Chomsky, Francis Fukuyama, Elizabeth Noelle-Neumann, Maxwell McCombs, Nicklas Luhmann, Jürgen Habermas, Manuel Castells, Roland Burkart, Cass Sunstein, and Dennis Mcquail. The book's hypotheses are based on these existing theories that apply to the new conditions online. The central thesis is that the economic policy model of online media is primarily based on the systematic manufacture of dissent. The principle of divide-and-rule in the online media of the 21st century is systematically applied. The Civil Cold War online is the business model of digital media, which adversely affects democratic processes in nation-states and undermines trust and social capital in societies.

A great example of the transition toward dissent in the mass media model is the research of the so-called Bad news. This line of media study was introduced in 1974 by the Glasgow University Media Group (GUMG), which pioneered the critical analysis of television news. GUMG founders Brian Winston, Greg Philo, and John Eldridge claimed that television news topics are biased in favor of the ruling classes of society. The study showed that the systematic bias and distortion of communication were over issues like climate change, conflicts like Israel/Palestine and Northern Ireland, welfare benefits, inequality, unions, economics, and refugees. GUMG's most popular publications are 'Bad News' in 1976 and 'More Bad News' in 1980. The second book develops the analytic findings and methods through a series of television news coverage case studies. It argues that the TV content reflects a highly partial viewpoint even simultaneously, the television programs are presented as balanced and factual news reporting. The surface appearance of neutrality turned out to be just propaganda from the establishment. The study is a classic example of 'manufacturing consent' as a part of the Propaganda model of 20th-century mass media. 'Bad news' research was almost forgotten until Routledge Revivals republished the book 'More Bad News'[2] in 2009. The idea is revived in the 2021 book 'Bad News: How Woke Media Is Undermining Democracy'[3] by Batya Ungar-Sargon. She argues that the identity culture war has allowed online media to divide American society along partisan and racial lines as a smokescreen for the actual division along class lines. As GUMG researchers 40 years ago, Ungar-Sargon sees how the media again is biased against the values and opinions of the working class. Journalism became an upper-class profession and turned its back to 'a truer chasm in American life—economic inequality.' The 40 years gap between the two books clearly shows the media model transition between the two centuries. Specific topics such as gender and race are partially excluded from the agenda of the democratic media in the late 20th century to prevent dissent and conflicts. Today, these topics are the leading newsworthy content in the global liberal media and attract as much attention as possible. In the new Propaganda 2.0 model of media, consent over the chasm of class and inequality is impossible, and it is replaced by the manufacture of dissent over ideological and racial topics. The Civil Cold War is an online ideological battle inside the public sphere of the state. That means even more bad news for global audiences and good news for online media businesses. This book aims to revitalise the ideas of Glasgow University Media Group and the traditions of Media criticism into the Fifth Estate of the Internet Realm.

Notes

1 Habermas, Jürgen. (1979). *Communication and the evolution of society.* Toronto: Beacon Press.
2 Beharrell, Peter, Howard Davis, John Eldridge, John Hewitt, Jean Hart, Gregg Philo, Paul Walton, and Brian Winston. (2009). *More bad news (Routledge revivals).* Abingdon, UK: Routledge.
3 Ungar-Sargon, B. (2021). *Bad news: How woke media is undermining democracy.* New York: Encounter Books.

Reference list

Beharrell, Peter, Howard Davis, John Eldridge, John Hewitt, Jean Hart, Gregg Philo, Paul Walton, & Brian Winston (2009). *More bad news (routledge revivals).* Abingdon, UK: Routledge.
Habermas, Jürgen (1979). *Communication and the evolution of society.* Toronto: Beacon Press.
Ungar-Sargon, B. (2021). *Bad news: How woke media is undermining democracy.* New York: Encounter Books.

1 Changing the paradigm of mass communication

Peter Ayolov

1.1. The need for a new paradigm

The advent of the manufacturing dissent model on the Internet results from changes in the global communication system and a lack of understanding of the new principles that govern it. In the 21st century, change was characterised by the relocation of centers and the transformation of the hierarchical structure for disseminating information. The old communication paradigm for transferring and filtering data from one center to all ends is irrelevant. This delay in understanding new trends in global communication processes leads to dysfunction in national systems and the creation of tensions and disagreements within countries. The discrepancy between the old paradigm of communication and the new reality of the Internet is one of the causes of crises in democracies.

The old paradigm is declining

In 2013, Dennis Mcquail's article 'Recreations on Paradigm Change in Communication Theory and Research'[1] was published. It calms all worries on the occasion of the impossibility of a general communication theory. Mcquail describes concerns about communication science's connections with power and business and awareness of the custom nature of research. The lack of a common view, principles, and a clear path for development is evident. Mcquail asks questions about the future of communication research and the necessary change. Why at all costs do we need a paradigm shift? What will we gain from this, and whether we should seek change as an end in itself? For Mcquail, it seems as if all parties are happy. Media merchants create a need for conspicuous consumption of junk news. Politicians form opinions and beliefs on a global scale. The audience consumes entertainment in any form and seems satisfied with it. The science of communication is also developing well, at least according to the quantity of research. It looks like none of the mass communication process participants are interested in changing the traditional paradigm. However, the change is happening right now, even if we can't describe it in new theories or terms. Internet media technology itself creates new perceptions of communication as a much broader social phenomenon. According to Mcquail, the main paradigm is in gradual decline, leading to the natural emergence of a new paradigm. The old 20th-century paradigm is characterised by an insurance of the newly created power of advertisers and propagandists and their ability to reach, more or less, the entire population simultaneously. This paradigm includes understanding the audience as the scattered crowd that gathers all individuals and unites them. Belief in the homogeneity of the audience creates a belief that the messages can be universal. It is believed that direct contact with each person is possible, bypassing the local culture, ideology, customs, family, religion, and politics. The old understanding of mass communication takes complete control of the content at the source for granted, leading to easily predictable effects and conformism desired by the state or any other form of power. Understanding communication, primarily as an efficient way to transfer information through technical means from one point to another, sounds outdated. Today, the Internet's computer network is mainly used to form new human communities. The Internet is, above all, an information space inhabited by digital avatars. Internet communication is characterised by group communication and the division of individuals into groups by shared views. The transfer of information is not an end in itself, and there is the role of uniting the people who share it. This group combination naturally implies some conflict and disagreement with other groups. Therefore, a universal communication model, simply as transmission, cannot be required anymore. The effect of communication is not only in data transportation but also in the transformation of human communities. Many communication studies have focused on the technical transmission of information and its use for control. Instead of looking for a replacement for this model, an alternative can be found to be used in parallel. The alternative must be sought in areas where communication theory lacks experience. In the traditional sense of mass communication, the media has become a powerful tool for control and management, although they should only be intermediaries. For Mcquail, this propaganda media model for mass control is characterised by public obedience being voluntary and often enthusiastic. In democracies, the propaganda suggestions of mass media are not openly imposed on individuals, as in totalitarian states. It is imperative to keep the feeling of personal choice. Instead of direct suggestions, mass messages create individual needs, desires, and inclinations in individual mass members. Since the beginning of the 20th century, the awe of great power and the power of advertising, PR, and propaganda in connection with the rapid development of communication technologies has begun. The peculiarities of this concept of mass communication are that the change in attitudes depends on the content that is sent and accepted. Media messages attack and take over traditional culture and break its filters, regulations, and rules. The media is becoming a key instrument of power with its almost instantaneous influence and control over people's minds. Individuals are considered only part of the mass, which can be 'formed' by the media, commissioned by the power elites, and big business.

The new paradigm

The new paradigm emerged in the late 20th century and has a different view of mass communication. It no longer has central control, but there are many channels, variety, and interactivity. The new communication paradigm turns several main pillars of the old, such as central control of messages from the center to the periphery. The distinctive features and main features of communication on the Internet, according to Mcquail, are as follows: Interactivity and messaging exchange, meanings, and roles; open and ready access to channels, to send and receive; 'multimediality'; lack of central management and control of the delivery and selection of information; unlimited capacity; low or insignificant costs for data transmission; end of territorial limitation (without a fixed place); diversity and constant flow of control, content, and applications; relative uncertainty in the direction, the meaning, and possible consequences. This change in the paradigm of technological development of mass communications and the entry of the Internet as a media is mainly related to the shift in thinking. The change follows the transition from an industrial to an information society and questions the basic principles of liberal democracy. The mathematical theory of communication as transmission and transportation of information is practical and liberally biased. A view of communication as a resource of power and a means of control is offered. The specter of artistic communication and ritual as a communication model is neglected in the name of a transport model. In 1975, James Carey spoke about this specter in his book 'A cultural approach to communication.' The new paradigm protects the idea that the roles of the sender and recipient can be changed. The leading goal of this process is the meaningful effect, whether it is desired or not. The primary function of this meaning is to unite the sender and the recipient and create shared values that create communities. In contrast to these new communities with equal access to information is the traditional linear communication model. He has his roots in religious, political, and economic propaganda of ideas. It is time for the elites who order this propaganda to decide whether to continue refining the methods of impact and control. Instead, they can pay attention to the side effects of propaganda. Such effects, such as the manufacture of dissent, lead to disturbances in the social system of norms and values. Harmful effects are social fragmentation and individual dysfunctions. The complete lack of control and misuse of public opinion leads to phenomena such as 'fake news,' 'post-truth,' 'truthiness,' and 'alternative facts.' These problems are formulated, and their negative impact leads to public imbalance. Internet technologies make it possible to gather information about these unwanted side effects of mass communication. That is why the elites themselves should be interested in supporting such research on the manufacture of dissent in the name of maintaining the status quo. The question is if the digital media giants as new elites will allow it.

The new media effects

The study of the effects of media impact became an essential topic of media research in the 21st century. All old theories are subject to revision. Mcquail focuses not on the motives or forecasts for a communication action, but on the actual consequences in specific communities and individuals. The audience is no longer seen as a relentless mass, but the complex picture of the effects of media messages is acknowledged. However, the idea of the total power of the mass media is being revived as a safe social mechanism, especially in social unrest and division. Theories of media hegemony face views of growing civic conscience and social criticism in the media. These theories attract many students and researchers in the 1970s and 1980s. They understand how little truth there is in the classic principles of journalistic objectivity. The reality is that media logic and the possibility of manipulation always precede the logic of truth and the ideas of the Enlightenment. The arguments for cultivation effects, agenda-setting, and spirals of silence paint a new picture. Mass media are seen as an organised system for manufacturing consent, manipulation, and social control. In a democracy, this media control can never be total and is always dependent on the audience. The effects on the media audience became the main subject of research. The complexity of influences on different individuals and various media content is considered. The Internet allows for a much better knowledge of audiences as a set of individuals, which leads to better and better mechanisms of media manipulation. On the other hand, the free sharing of information on social networks returns to seeing communication as a ritual for creating human communities. Strong communities do not need media and are made up of people who directly connect. For them, the media is just a space for exchanging information. Today, the Internet takes the place of shared space as an open market for ideas and opinions. This open communication complements the hypothesis of powerful media with other areas of the theory as a broad constructivist view. According to this view, news agencies and other media sources produced the media coverage of events under external pressure. As a result, according to various perceptions and interests, the message is subject to differentiated understanding by the audience. Such an approach includes an extended concept of the leading media effect and accepts different types of impact and new research methods. Understanding the audience as a mass dies hard because it has been conveniently used in the media system of advertising and propaganda for many years. Today, more and more people are thought of as an active, self-determining, and interpretive community. It is impossible to predict all the effects of mass communication, but conclusions can be drawn about changing trends. Collecting data for each individual and storing them in digital archives leads to this new understanding. Today, audiences are active, and constant change is registered through constant online observation. In the past, due to a lack of technology for such continuous monitoring, it is concluded that it is as if the audience can only be as the media and sociological research imagine it. If the audience is perceived as a homogeneous mass, 'manufacturing consent' is applied through an organised propaganda campaign. The appropriate control strategy is divide-and-rule if the audience is perceived as a community of independent and interpretive people. The mass is divided into warring groups and thus is mastered by the whole. The divide-and-online rule model finds ideal ground for development on the Internet. The issue of attitudes toward the public is moral and is key to the scientific approach to media research in democracies. In a democracy, the power elite does not have trust and respect for most individuals, and it treats them as a mass of consumers. That makes the very idea of democracy meaningless. Then, it is natural that businesses and private corporations do better to meet consumer needs. On the other hand, trust in the wisdom of public opinion is at the heart of a democratic state. The study of the effects on media audiences acknowledges this trust, and the model for a mass audience is abandoned. Terms are introduced for 'consulting' and 'conversing' audiences. The old image of the audience as an anonymous set, convenient for manipulation by media owners, is still alive. This image is practically useful for media designers, advertisers, marketing, influencers, communicators, and information merchants.

The new audiences

New audiences are not as geographically localised and homogeneous as old ones. Through the various social networks on the Internet, individuals become 'intercommunicators' associated with many other people and circles. New research even mentions the death of the public or rediscovering the people. There is a mixture of personal, public, and professional communication, but the main feature of the new audiences is that they are scattered or 'Dispersed.' The question is, once the audiences are scattered, then can public opinion exist at all? Austrian scientist Roland Burkart used the term 'Dispersive audience' in his 1998 book 'Communication Science'[2] (Kommunikationswissenschaft). This dispersive audience has common opinions and interests, but it does not represent a community. The dispersed audience has a 'non-public opinion.' The new audiences consist of individuals who are only connected because they are interested in a message from the mass media. Instead of human communities, dispersive audiences in the Internet media create networks of individuals. Their unification is more of the principles of the flock or swarm than of consent and understanding in human society. Dispersive audiences are not long-term social education but always arise as appropriate. There are no direct interpersonal relationships between members of such a dispersal audience. Usually, recipients are divided and anonymous and only know that many others perceive the same message.

Burkart calls into question the very essence of mass communication and the need for reciprocity and community-building for the existence of the human touch. For Burkart, this is reminiscent of the ideas of the communication myth. Isn't mass communication mass journalism? Communication cannot be one-sided; it requires reciprocity. In a continuous publication and comment, communication between personalities is no longer occurring. Communication becomes automatic and ritual. Communication actions are just habits. The complex question of media effects has no unequivocal answer. The constant research change also requires a constant flux of methods and approaches. According to Burkart, the effects of mass media are like a bottomless barrel. The problems in mass communication can be understood by studying the groups and communities that people create because it reveals their social nature. The Internet and social networks give a unique chance to explore this nature and the natural desire of individuals to create groups of all kinds. Although the Internet is a new media, it unites all traditional mass media in one. Then, the validity of all theories and hypotheses of mass communication must be checked on the Internet. The emergence of dispersive audiences who create non-public opinions begins with the disintegration of the large family and the intimate, spontaneous communication between people. An increasing and complex system of society requires a growing organisation, which is at the expense of personal and immediate contact. Thus, non-public opinion is simply a sum of the same opinions of a group of individuals and does not produce a human community. It turns out that in the process of industrialisation and democratisation of society, the 'primary groups' have survived. They offer individual external social stabilisation. These primary groups are the family, the circle of friends, the neighborhood, and the rural municipalities. They are intimate, direct, personal, and emotional. Accepting large groups of people as a mass or crowd facilitates communication research and simplifies results. Modern technical means for monitoring and recording the actions of individuals on the Internet provide a new opportunity for research. It is possible to create more detailed geographical maps of human relationships, such as members of groups and communities. Internet media publications do not consist of a mass of atomized and isolated individuals. Instead, they are divided into interconnected small groups. The image of the audience, like a uniform mass divided by a dozen criteria, was created and imposed by traditional mass media. There was no technical possibility for feedback and audience research in detail. Internet posts are active and interconnected, but these links are dynamic. The connections, dependencies, and influences between individuals and groups turn out to be much more important in forming public opinion than the media message itself. For Burkart, the study of this network of groups and connections is at the heart of understanding the new paradigm for forming public opinion. In people's political decisions, the value of interpersonal communication is growing. Other individuals influence people more than the media.

The new research

The influence of groups and leaders of public opinion on the Internet is growing, and traditional media lose power over the masses. Public confidence in the media is declining at the expense of following charismatic leaders. Mass media is much more appropriate to strengthen than to change their minds, and in many cases, their effect is zero. This media failure is becoming an increasingly important issue for research into mass communication. The question 'Why?' about the motivation and effects of media messages is on the agenda. Roland Burkart raises the question of the public interest in the use of mass media. The question 'What do people do with the media?'[3] demonstrates the reality of mass communication. The impact of the mass media becomes a question of the use of the news that the media reports. The direction of communication research shifts from mechanistic bias to empirical research. These mathematical theories and research are easy to manipulate. They are presented as media events and are used by influencers and 'would-be persuaders.' They ignore important social and cultural factors of influence and persuasion. Neglected is any phenomenon that cannot be accurately measured, packaged, and sold. For example, these are beliefs and beliefs such as individual experience and philosophy. In addition, empirical research cannot cover all mods, tastes, moods, opinions, attachments, loyalty, social and revolutionary movements, models of connectivity and communication, public debates, and conversations about vital topics. Traditional research faces the obvious difficulty and impossibility of accurately accounting for these phenomena and characteristics. But a more optimistic view of the new paradigm of communication science shows that communication today is more open, organic, and generates ideas. Communication with connectivity and feedback between the participants. Each participant will be an author and an audience in future mass journalism. In this communication spiral of constant sharing and comments, manipulation is possible but also seems to be voluntarily accepted. It stems from the very relationship of dependence and bias between the participants rather than from some effect of the media message. The participants in the communication action are biased toward an opinion, rather because of loyalty to the group, instead of deep beliefs and access to facts. This bias is sought after, and manipulation in friendly groups is accepted with anticipation. Thus, with the focus on virtual communities, the concept of the effects of mass media gradually becomes redundant. New digital technologies provide an opportunity for comprehensive monitoring and measurement of communication processes, which has not been possible in the past. It requires a special accuracy for the details and relationships of the new type of research. The aim is not to test pre-imposed ideas but to understand and support the natural process of creating and destroying human communities. Only when the disintegration of old public communication systems is understood can new and better be built. The inertia of the old model of mass communication requires the manufacture of dissent with all its negative effects. Unfortunately, the new possibilities of technology for comprehensive monitoring of human habits are mainly used by private and business interests. That also applies to biased and commissioned media research, which grows every year. Businesses have traditionally navigated much faster in the new paradigm and used changes in demand for profit. State and public organisations lag in the use of new communication technologies. This new e-government in traditional nation-states hopes to change the paradigm of mass communication. The e-government is not just a technology but a project for a future public contract that produces consent and social order with the help of machines. There is hope that the e-government is a possible solution to the crises of disagreement in democratic societies. Computer algorithms seem like the last hope to solve the problem of disinformation, conflict propaganda, false news, and systematic distortion of information. According to Dennis Mcquail,[4] it will be difficult to change the paradigm because the old models are still working well. Many influential people in advertising and the media will continue to use them to the end. The audience also does not seem interested in any general change. The question is, who needs the new paradigm? The responsibility lies with communication researchers. They must feel the dynamics of changing themselves and follow it with their research. Every important scientific idea is considered important precisely because it has met the requirements of the spirit of the time in which it is used. Every time gives birth to its ideas and creates its world. In the history of science, it often happens that the latest discoveries are found in the oldest theories. The discoverer is the one who manages to cross a bridge over time. Technological changes are not enough to change the paradigm, but 'directions for the development of a new and broader understanding of communication are noted and are still piling up.' The theory of communication must be adapted to changes in its subject and require a change in the paradigm of communication. If the trends this book traces turn out to be true, understanding communication as a transmission of information must be abandoned. The new understanding being shaped is more like a ritual for creating and maintaining communities. The manufacture of dissent is a threat precisely to understanding in traditional human communities. The new paradigm for studying communication must also focus on this organised division of people. Wide access to information and research on the Internet enables everyone to research communication and its effects. Equality and communication between communication researchers are crucial for change. The communication paradigm of domination and power must be overcome. Imposing a new information order is an old idea that is possible with the advent of the Internet.

1.2. The rise of dissent in the network society

The advent of the Internet, particularly the emergence of the so-called Web 2 or Web.2.0, took place at a 2004 conference Web 2.0 Summit in San Francisco. It marks the beginning of creating a new second-generation computer network in which consumers are free to communicate and associate with each other. This network we call the Internet is not just new media, such as the printed book, the newspaper, the radio, the phone, and the television. The Internet is a communication network in which information is interconnected semantically. This information is general and accessible and is constantly supplemented. The Semantic Web is the term used by network creator Tim Berners-Lee. The ultimate goal of the Internet is a network of interconnected data. The connections and indices with which it is archived quickly do the semantic search for information. In addition, Web 2.0 completely reversed the ways and ideas of creating and maintaining human communities. As people are free to create news and share it, the media is becoming increasingly redundant. It's the beginning of a lasting trend of 'disintermediation,' a process known in the economy as 'to cut out the middle man.' This trend leads irreversibly to a reduction in confidence in large and established media channels. They are looking for new media and social networks with different content and audiences. An extreme phase of disintegration occurs when everyone can create their information channel on the Internet's social networks.

'Mediocratia'

The disintegration processes online cultivate individualism and narcissism, creating an atmosphere of disagreement between individuals searching for personal affirmation at the expense of the collective spirit. The Internet media form public opinion, but this opinion creates a sense of community and belonging only in a certain virtual group. This 'non-public opinion' online is different from public opinion within the nation-state. The Internet enables the creation of many groups and many opinions that are reluctant to merge in the name of national understanding and agreement. Thus, the very essence of the Internet presupposes a communication model of disagreement. This disagreement ultimately pushes society to change because of the discovery of differences and inequality between individuals. Unlike the pseudo-agreement produced, disagreement leads to discovering power inequality and conflict. Social control, which is achieved based on the principle of divide-and-rule online, is short-lived. Spontaneous disagreement is a valuable social mechanism and cannot be imitated successfully. Any attempt at false 'manufacturing' is a pseudo-communication and imitation of spontaneous human relationships. Public expression of disagreement is at the heart of democracy, but it must be spontaneous, not a reaction to external suggestions. In democracies, one can freely choose what groups and communities to participate in according to consent or dissent with the opinions of other members. On the Internet, reaching an agreement in a group is becoming increasingly difficult because of the ease with which each member can create a new group of dissenters with the senior leadership. There is a process of constant disagreement and division, which is not a free and natural process.

The division is in the interest of digital companies that manage virtual spaces on the Internet. It is an artificial interference in the spontaneous communication processes with strongly negative social effects. In the manufacturing dissent model, the media also are interested in seeking conflict and disagreement as an effect of their publications. The escalation of conflict in Internet media through conflict propaganda is becoming a media model. In it, the basic principle is 'Angry people click more.' The Internet is a virtual market that sells people's emotional reactions. The 'click' or touch has commercial value and is for sale. This click acquires the power to vote or cast the ballot in political elections. A new type of digital consent is governed in a new type of virtual state. Such an online vote gives power to transnational corporations and global businesses. They are more influential than political parties and entire countries in many cases. International corporations own much of the mass media, becoming increasingly independent of state regulation. As a result, local institutions lose control of forming public opinion. Thus, voting in political elections is beginning to have less and less value than click voting. Technology companies control the technologies for forming public opinion. This control gives real political power to the hands of mass media and social networks. In their interest, they may decide whether to produce consent or disagreement. A government by media or 'Mediocratia'[5] (Das Mediokratie) is required, as defined by Ulrich von Alemann. Mediocratia means that the media is the fourth estate and obeys its own rules and laws. If democracy has become a television democracy in the past, then the mediocracy of the Internet and social networks is complete control of the public space. It is no coincidence that there is already serious talk of e-government and an internet democracy. In democracies, the power to form public opinion is the supreme power that rules the state itself. In the struggle for this power, the media naturally strive to pit people against each other through hostile ideologies and causes. In the absence of regulation, this process intensifies and weakens national ideologies in the conditions of online media. One of the basic principles of 'mediocratia' on the Internet is the manufacturing of dissent. An ongoing war of opinion between different communities favors the media. Their conflict guarantees the audience and profits. The manufacture of the dissent model is the economic policy of online media. What does the fourth power of the media mean today? The mediator's power is the power of control over the information channels. The position of the mediator is not creative, and there is no creative energy to create social values. The media can only transfer these values between groups and individuals. Attempts by intermediaries to create content of public value are always mediocre. Marshall McLuhan warns about the effects of electronic media, such as a branch of the nervous system of humanity. The media is a message without an author. A ready-made communication or information garbage. The author is connected to the community on behalf of which he writes, while the mediator has no interests related to the community. Presumably, traders have interlocal interests. The media, as traders of information, have global interests. The technology of digital media itself relies on the transmission and reception of information at any point on the planet. Thus, the location of the media is not just the address where the office is registered. 'The media is the message' means that the media itself is a flux of information. The media is a casual relationship between people, while the community is the genetic link. In the primary human community, communication is direct and without intermediaries. Unity is based on strict rules and taboos on what and how it can be discussed. Self-censorship is at the heart of any stable human community. The media and the community are in natural enmity. Interestingly, in English, the term 'Mediocratia,' which uses Aleman instead of government by media, can be translated as 'mediocracy.' It means a system with a dominant class consisting of mediocre people or a system in which mediocrity is rewarded. In English, there is a natural link between the word 'media' in the sense of 'environment' and the word 'mediocre' in the sense of 'mediocre, medium, bad, medium quality.' It can be said that the system of domination and power of the media has mediocre results and a negative impact on communities. It is in the media's interest to reduce trust between individuals and social capital. The media traded in medium-based information and targeted the average person as an audience. In the search for ever-broader audiences, the media became servants of the primary passions of the mass audience. An audience that they create and maintain. The 'Mediocratia' model on the Internet realises Walter Lippmann's worst fears about the power of the bewildered herd. 'A phantom public,' which cannot make its own decisions and make sensible plans. The problem on the Internet is with the educated elite, which Lippmann says should manage the media. This elite is also part of this new virtual mass of would-be persuaders and information sellers. The economic policy of online media works with blind automatism, despite the intentions of the elites. The possibility of information equality and a new world information order is threatened. The global model of manufacturing dissent is subject to market principles and treats human emotions and communities only as a commodity.

Media ecology

At the beginning of the 21st century, research on new media on the Internet is still searching for a new theory. One of the media theories interested in the effects on society when new technologies enter is Media Ecology. This discipline addresses how the means of mass communication affect human perception, beliefs, and behaviors. How does our interaction in the 'media space' facilitate or hinder our chances of survival over time? The word 'Ecology' is used in the sense of 'house, home, space and environment' (from Greek: -οἶκος, 'house,' or 'environment' and -λογία, 'study of'). According to Neil Postman,[6] media ecology deals with studying the media as a familiar space. The media serves as a new home for our perceptions, understandings, feelings, and values. It is the environment that structures what we can see and say. Therefore, this space also determines what we can do. The media assigns us social roles and insists that we play them in public. The media decides what is allowed to be done and what is not, which equates the role of the media with that of public opinion. The media are the technology and territory for creating public opinion and morality. They replace human communities and take on their responsibilities. In cases of a strongly negative effect on society, the task of media ecology is to reveal that behind the illusion of an independent mediator is a machine of suggestions. Media Ecology is trying to understand what roles we are forced to play in the media environment. Why the media makes us feel and act in a certain way? The media ecology approach is suitable for studying the manufacturing dissent model. One of the creators of this direction of communication theory is Marshall McLuhan imposes the term 'media ecology' in his book 'Understanding media'[7] of 1964. As a leading specialist in this field, UNESCO has invited McLuhan as a member of the International Commission for Communication Problems. This commission explored the problems of mass communication and the need for a new world information order. Unfortunately, he could not join the commission because of a serious illness that led to his death in 1980. Eight years later, his son Eric McLuhan published their joint book, 'Laws of Media,' which presents the hypothesis of 'The Four of Media Effects.' According to McLuhan, these are the four primary effects of any new technology and media on society. These effects are the answers to the questions: What 'Increases'? (Enhances); What is 'Disposed of use'? (Obsoletes); What 'Rolls and leads to extremes'? (Reverses), and What 'Get Out of Forget'? (Retrieves). A quick attempt to apply The Four Media Effects to the Internet as a new media may seem like this:

- The Internet Enhances: decentralisation, criticism and disagreement, access to information, facilitates interpersonal communication, facilitates associative demand, freedom of choice, self-expression, the possibility of publication, the connection with world media, global concerns, immediacy, saving time, virtual communities, e-commerce, etc.
- The Internet Obsoletes: the boundaries between countries, the direct connection between people, the invariability of information and history, monopolies, official propaganda, censorship, printing, and more.
- The Internet Reverses: isolation, information overload, lack of real people and stories, lack of absolute truth, life in virtual worlds, insensitivity, nervous disorders, moral panic, and general consent in a great society now become a model of disagreement from tribal culture
- The Internet Retrieves: tribes and villages in small virtual communities, anarchy, chaos, writing and correspondence, local activism, and others.

According to McLuhan's famous expression, the media changes the 'message' and how we live. The intermediary's interest is in every message it carries. Thus, he suggests his point of view on the recipient. The use of one or another media impacts the reality of the individual. The politician who uses the radio is completely different from the one who uses television. Today, more and more politicians use the Internet and social networks as media which completely changes the political system. The four media effects of the Internet are yet to lead to changes in all spheres of social life. Especially in creating communities and connections between them. McLuhan predicts the future of virtual communities on the Internet and calls it the 'Global village,' a virtual space made up of small interconnected communities. These new global communities are restricted by geographical location, state, and national affiliation. These develop in parallel with local communities but are not limited by distances, borders, traditions, and laws. They manage to reproduce precisely on the Internet in conditions of constant disagreement. Thus, democratic consent manufacturing becomes impossible.

The new virtual space offers an infinite place to express all opinions, an apparent realisation of individual desires. It seems that the eternal shortage and territorial limitations of the material world have been overcome. In the virtual world, dissent is a creative force that encourages individuals dissatisfied with the status quo to create new and new communities. Every new conflict leads to division due to the unlimited virtual space on the Internet. Similar opinions coexist in an agreement sealed by battles with hostile groups. Technology companies use filters to keep consent inside small groups. A 'filter bubble' is insulation that occurs if websites use algorithms to select the information that the user would like to see. These assumptions are based on previous user behavior, such as browsing and clicking history, search history and location, etc. After a dissent has been manufactured, it is ensured that the consumer will observe his previous activity. In short, his behavior will be predictable. In addition to filter balloons, there are other forms of intellectual self-isolation and systematically distorted communication. These are the 'echo chambers' and the 'epistemic bubbles.' The epistemic bubble is a social epistemic structure in which external voices are missed. The echo chamber is a social epistemic structure where external voices are discredited. Members of epistemic balloons are simply not exposed to any information or arguments. The members of the echo chambers are brought to systematic distrust of all external sources. No other voices are heard in epistemic balloons, while others are actively undermined in the echo chambers. These are just some of the effects of the Global village and the divide-and-rule online model. Systematic division of people with different opinions who can live in the same city but are divided into virtual spaces.

The future of the Internet

The development of the Internet and digital information technologies has an increasing impact on policy and social planning. Ideas are born to use artificial intelligence to regulate human relationships and create an e-government parallel with actual state structures. Businesses are the first to respond to these changes. There are already positive examples of the effects of the Internet, such as the sharing economy. The ideology of this new economy of network sharing does not seek profit at any cost before building networks of trust between users. It makes full use of all accessible spaces, resources, and services. This type of communication network excludes intermediaries and connects all individuals directly. The goal is a fair and equitable system for distributing information, resources, goods, and services regulated independently of a computer algorithm. Of course, the practice of a shared economy is different from this ideal. Over time, it remains to be tested whether this system can control the destructive effects of pursuing profit at any cost. If the shared economy model works, then shared governance can also be discussed in the future. It would increase political stability, economic efficiency, and social capital. McLuhan's idea of a global village in the age of the Internet is to restore the proximity and unity of the rural municipality in a global interconnected network. People want to feel the closeness of the people around them, but at the same time be connected through personal information channels to the whole world. This model of a future virtual democracy and e-government is the most optimistic view of the future. The trends are for the development of the Internet as a total communication system uniting the economy, culture, education, politics, and finance. The entry of WEB 3.0 or the so-called Semantic Web and Internet of Things (IoT) clearly shows the direction for the development of the social sphere and mass communication. The third generation of the Internet, or the 'Semantic Network,' is based on a hierarchical arrangement of information in the so-called Semantic Web Stacks information bundles. This model replaces the current Internet system, dominated by unstructured data networks.

The future of the Internet depends on the possibilities for ensuring the reliability of the information. It is no coincidence that 'Trust' is placed at the top in hierarchically arranged layers of Semantic Web Stacks. It is above the layer of 'Proof' and 'Logic.' The goals and principles for developing future communication systems must be built on trust as a higher social value. In addition, there is already talk about the origin of the information or 'Provenance.' Provenance from French provenir, 'to come from/forward,' is the history of a historical site's ownership, custody, or location. 'Provenance of information' is crucial for deciding how much information should be trusted. The moral principles of communication always catch up with technology. Communication technology is ahead of social progress and the development of the general ethical principles of humanism. One of these universal principles is trust between individuals and the tendency to create communities born of it. This principle of trust is also valid on the Internet. Semantic Web development or WEB 3.0 attempts to put it into practice. The aim of researchers in this area should be to develop a Web of Trust that combines the achievements of technology with ethical ideals and the principles of humanism.

The reality of the network society

The reality of the development of online communication is very different from technological utopias in the recent past. Trends are instead for the Internet to repeat the adverse effects in the development of other media technologies in the past. Online media and social networks are increasingly becoming spaces for conflict and war of ideas. Impermanent relationships between people with different social statuses and a communication culture lead to constant instability and tension. In addition, the Internet contributes to growing economic and information inequality in the world. Manuel Castells further developed Marshall McLuhan's ideas in his book 'The Rise of the Network Society.' Instead of global villages worldwide, we live in personalised villas produced globally and distributed locally. In this information age, culture has displaced nature and is independent of the material foundations of human existence. Every value and power in this new communication order is based on the connections with the network. The proximity to large information flows and global metropolises as nodes in this network is defining. Individuals living in these personalised electronic villas have the unique opportunity to share personal opinions on all issues. They freely create connections and communities with other individuals connected to the global network, which naturally tests traditional society in the nation-state. The relationships between individuals and groups determine the structure of power. People are increasingly breaking away from the problems of local communities and life at the local level. They begin to create their values and emotional contacts in virtual spaces. For more and more people, the media is indeed an expression of our culture. For Castells, this culture, in turn, is based primarily on the content or material provided by the media. The big news on the Internet allows audiences to be truly interactive. Individuals can be involved in the communication process as content authors. This infinite variety of content also creates the preconditions for a growing disagreement in traditional communities. Traditional narratives that unite individuals lose their strength. New technologies lead to an evolution from a mass to a segmented society. A system with increasingly specialised and personal information is needed. Such information targeting does not have the power to unite people in large groups. The diversification goes so far as to create different media for different types of information and leads to so-called filter bubbles as one way of manufacturing dissent.

While television forms the language of public communication in the past, there are thousands of different online languages today. Virtual Babylon divides people into millions of new groups, regardless of the classic divisions according to geography, culture, ideology, ethnicity, language, and nationality. Castells speaks of a completely new 'culture of real virtuality' that emerges and in which there is no difference between reality and symbolic representation. A culture that exists only through mass communication between millions of people. Unlike local communities, the connections created in virtual communities are weak and volatile. Online communication is also more candid, leading to controversy, scandals, and insults. Individuals are forced to maintain relationships in the family and the circle of friends despite disagreements. In traditional communication, there is a complex system of self-censorship, taboos, and euphemization to guarantee consent. Communication without any reservations is something completely unpredictable. Even an insulting word can leave the group or end the relationship in virtual communities. Manuel Castells believes that 'Computer-mediated communication' (CMC) causes tension and disagreement between the culture of narcissism and the community dreams of each individual. CMC networks have technologically defined properties of individualization and interactivity. The communities become more unstable and prone to disintegration and division. On the other hand, virtual communities have a more egalitarian communication pattern than traditional local structures. Social classes are much less important in creating relationships between individuals.

A false sense of authority in specific individuals is created on the Internet. Hidden behind the anonymity of the profile, they play a social role they would like to have in real life. The false sense of social mobility has only virtual value. Since there is no established system for building social authority and class division, conflicts and disagreements are natural. Virtual communities follow the trend of 'privatization of communication.' Social connections are rebuilt around individuals, and this leads to division. Smaller groups with clear leaders are being created. Castells makes an interesting observation about the released spontaneous communication in the early years of the Internet. At the end of the 20th century, the symbolism of power had not yet discovered its language in historically new media. The change is rapid, and today the Internet is becoming an instrument of state and corporate power. An interesting observation is that the new media do not move away from traditional cultures, but usually they swallow them. The old power structures are implemented in the new communication systems and follow the same principles. This concentration of power and the differentiation and segmentation of audiences make possible the divide-and-rule model on the Internet.

The empty shell of democracy

The growing information inequality and social stratification divide the world into active and passive participants in the network society. The current structures of power are preserved. Despite another promise of egalitarianism in the network society, inequality is rising. Once again, this leads to disagreement, social cataclysms, and state crises. Changes in the paradigm of communication always lead to changes in the political system. The manufacturing dissent model as a policy strategy is one of the indicators for these changes. In the second volume of his book 'The Power of Identity,'[8] Manuel Castells spoke of 'the politics of scandal' as a model of political communication based on dissent. The main task of politics today is to make a public appearance. Media dramatisation of messages is especially important. The deliberate search for disagreement and conflict with political opponents works for the benefit of both sides. This politics of scandal is increasingly being transferred to the Internet. Since media is the space of politics in the information age, politics is also part of the culture of real virtuality. Politics relies more on media presentation of artificially imposed topics than seeking consensus and solving real problems. Anyone who wants to attract more attention must dramatise their message and provoke moral anger. The politics of scandal aims at a continuous flow of scandalous topics and becomes a model of political dramatisation. The conflict is heated until it subsides and is replaced by a new one. The goal is total conquest of the public. Thus, Manuel Castells clearly describes the manufacturing dissent model in the political system. Only yellow newspapers did this due to media regulation, journalistic ethics, and censorship in the past. Today, the freedom of online media makes them an ideal space for this constant scandalous war that leads to a loss of confidence in the entire political system. It is based mainly on conflict and moves in inertia, without purpose and direction. The crisis of confidence in the political system is added to the 'crisis of legitimacy' of the nation-state. The party system is reduced to simply an open competition between the political parties in the media arena. Internet age policy has been reduced to personalised leadership. It is highly dependent on technological means of manipulation, a memory of a glorious past with a bureaucratic remnant devoid of public trust. Castells ends with the fact that despite a lack of trust in democracy, people accept the system of competition, disagreement, and scandal. According to Churchill, democracy is the worst form of government—except for all the others tried. The current regime of competing policies is not an adequate mechanism of political representation in the network society. People feel it in their collective memory, but they know how important it is to prevent tyrants from taking up the space free of democracy. Those who remember the horrors of wars and totalitarianism, which always comes to fill the gap after democracy, are still alive.

For Manuel Castells, that democracy, as it was born of liberal revolutions in the 19th century and spread around the world in the 20th century, has become an 'empty shell.' In a global network society, citizens are still citizens, but without a city. In the age of the Internet, the dissent model turns out to be the only working political model that makes any sense. It is done not by instilling faith in a particular ideology, but by opposing two or more content-washed banal ideas. Thus, the meaning is created in the very clash of conflicting opinions. Disagreements with hostile ideology become an act of identification. Media research on this pathological system of dissent is still in its infancy. Ways are being sought to transform online conflict into a network of understanding and social progress. A similar idea is the UNESCO New World Information Order project.

1.3. The 'New World Information Order' dystopia

Digital media and information archiving and analysis technologies make a detailed map of global communication processes possible. A new atlas of the worldwide information order is being created, and considerable information inequality is coming to light. This inequality is systematic and progressive. It is supported by a total system for allocating world information. It can be said that we are witnessing new information totalitarianism. When human communication is seen only as a transmission, it can transmit impersonal orders and commands. In the new communication paradigm, a sense of reciprocity is shared instead of commands. This paradigm illuminates traditional hierarchical systems of power and inequality, so they lose their strength. Communication is understood as maintaining communities of equal and informed individuals. Sharing creates, above all, equality of awareness and communication in knowledge. It is the only direction of communication that guarantees reciprocity, trust, creativity, and social progress.

Information inequality

In the 1970s, at several meetings organised by UNESCO and the 'Non-Aligned Movement,' was created the idea for a 'New World Information and Communication Order' (NWICO). In 1977, UNESCO's secretary-General Amadou-Mahtar M'Bow commissioned Nobel Peace Prize winner Sean MacBride to set up an 'International Commission for the Study of Communication Problems.' In 1981 the commission published a report, known as the MacBride Report[9] under the name 'Communication and Society Today and Tomorrow, Many Voices One World, Towards a new more just and more efficient world information and communication order.' This report makes a highly accurate analysis of the problems in global communication at the end of the 20th century. It is planned to create a new, more equal, and open communication network. Access to information and the possibility of communication with other people with shared interests is the basis of social progress. That must be the goal of the international community, UNESCO, and the United Nations. The MacBride report identifies the pattern of dominance in communication and power centralization as a major source of social and information inequality. Information inequality and limited communication lead to social apathy and helplessness, which prevent individuals and communities from all points on Earth from fully developing their potential. The Many Voices One World report warns of the dangers of the concentration of 'information power' and possible dysfunction in the communication system. There is a risk that new technologies will make communication systems even more rigid and increase their 'dysfunctions.' Media monopolies are established, and there is a danger of growing imbalances, inequality, and a sense of irresponsibility and helplessness.

In 1980, the MacBride report recommended the creation of a global information bank of computers connected to a network of what we call the Internet today. It is not a prediction of a science fiction novel but an official UNESCO report. The authors were a group of specialists in communications worldwide, including representatives of the United States and the USSR. One of the most famous representatives of the commission was the Colombian writer Gabriel Garcia Marquez. Special attention is paid to the risk of limiting the ability of poor countries to access information. That could increase the existing contradictions between the growing dependence of the countries and their national independence. The report emphasises the crucial importance of the ways and moral principles of the new informatics technology. Like any other tool, computers can be a 'servant or master.' On the one hand, they can exacerbate power problems and communication inequality to the extreme. Computers can make society more hierarchical and bureaucratic and boost technocracy and centralization. On the other hand, they can make social life more accessible, spontaneous, open, and democratic. They can protect the diversity of decision-making through different media and sharing technologies. The most important thing is to realise the danger of dehumanising communication. After all, it all depends on how society wants to use any new communication technology. In this regard, the MacBride Commission shows a rare example in the international community of will and joint action to change. A timely warning about social and moral consequences of digital media entry. The need for the humanization of mass communication is indicated. Instead of enormous mass audiences, a network of interconnected individuals is created. Communication equality and access to information destroy power control systems. Interpersonal communication on a global scale is a guarantee of reaching an agreement between people. A consensus that overcomes the stereotypes of groups in a spontaneous and open discussion. People have no choice but to communicate and achieve a 'universal understanding' of each other. The MacBride report also addresses a fundamental issue of international organisations such as the United Nations; they do not have their official media. When an international institution relies on external media, its connection with people is through an intermediary. That raises the question of the power of media monopolies internationally to legitimise global control. Only free and open communication gives the public the power to get involved directly in policy-making. The media received enormous power as intermediaries of the relationship between those in power and individuals. The control of a small group of countries and private business interests in global mass media is always biased. This information monopoly is dangerous for balance in international understanding and peace. The position of the MacBride Report is that a new global communication system can help create an 'International Public Opinion.' This means a fundamental step toward creating a global community between all peoples. People themselves agree on important issues instead of consent manufactured by the international elites and suggested through their mass media. Creating conditions for an 'international public opinion' can guarantee lasting peace and understanding. The United Nations must consider creating an auxiliary global information system capable of giving voice to this international public opinion.

In 1980, The MacBride report saw the lack of an independent global communication system as a paradox. A system democratically controlled by the international community and meets the whole world's needs. It is difficult for the commission to accept that the international community does not have its media. Its creation is, before all, a matter of a new morality rather than of technology and political will. It is vital to stimulate and engage connections and cooperatives with existing media. Without such a system, it is impossible to create new values from which new ethics can be born. Today, the idea and desire for this new morality exist in the Internet media. One can see the willingness of different organisations for the free and equal dissemination of information, which gives hope for implementing the MacBride report and UNESCO recommendations.

International public opinion

The MacBride report also raises the question of the possibility of the media imposing a specific opinion on the public, which creates apathy in the citizens and kills the spirit of democracy. The imposition of a non-public opinion constructed by the mass media favors particular interests is contrary to the spirit of democracy. The agreement is reached in the clash of different opinions that is the structure of the democratic process. On the one hand, the media provides the audience with information beyond possible direct experience. But people themselves must construct public opinion in consensus instead of taking it from the media. This social apathy does not support democracy, which cannot exist without the participation of citizens. Public opinion cannot reflect the content of the mass media. In the democratic process, discussions and the pursuit of understanding are crucial to decision-making. Despite the global dominance of the Internet, today, we cannot talk about international public opinion. Such a global consensus is lacking even on critical issues, for example, the fight against climate change or the need for vaccination. The difficulty in reaching an agreement comes from the lack of desire of the international community, especially those countries that have information supremacy. The divide-and-rule model works well, and the status quo has no interest in changing the communication system. The other difficulty in creating international public opinion is the lack of global media to represent the United Nations. The media is how public opinion is formed, and different opinions are created. International public opinion cannot appear on its own. It must be a child of the merging of national beliefs. Governments are increasingly registering and complying with views in their own countries and worldwide. Creating a global opinion begins with an ordinary consciousness and common sympathy between people. It should not be the global manufacture of consensus. In an ideal form, world public opinion must be created equal dialogue—a multidirectional flow of information between all countries, groups, and individuals who compile the opinion. Social networks of the Internet allow for this type of community in which individuals are in constant contact. Then public opinion exists somewhat in the public consciousness with ordinary morality. Whether it is a utopia to believe that such a relationship is possible will show the future. According to the MacBride Report, only the creation of such a shared consciousness gives the right audience not only to have an opinion but also to judge. Only the power of unity and the community's consent can legitimise the control over the individual. Sooner or later, every other power loses its reason because it does not support a single human society. The main conclusion of the MacBride Report is related to the future effects of horizontal, humane, and democratic communication. These effects are in the development and use of the full potential of all individuals in the world. People are treated not as objects but as creators of ideas and active agents of social development. The New Information Order aims to fight for the transformation of the audience from passive viewers into active actors in their own lives.

Today the MacBride report remains just a dream, but many of the tips and prescriptions for the New Information Order are beginning to be performed entirely spontaneously. Proof of the foresight and moral position on studying communication problems by Nobel Peace Prize winner Sean MacBride and UNESCO's Communication Commission. The report is an example of the difficulties facing any attempt to change the pattern of domination and power in communication. One reason is that mass communication is the basis of financial and military power. It is the control of communications that guarantees the legitimacy of this power. A new information order threatens developed Western countries' established inequality and dominance over mass communication. Some of the conclusions and prescriptions of the MacBride Commission sound very dangerous for the establishment: (1) Elimination of information inequality; (2) Excluding the negative impact of monopolies; (3) Free flow of news; (4) More sources and channels of information; (5) Freedom and responsibility of journalists; (6) Improving the capacity of developing countries; (7) Freedom of the press information; (8) Sincere will to help developing countries; (9) Respect for cultural identity; (10) Respect for all peoples in information exchange; (11) Right to access the sources of information for groups and individuals. Shortly after the report was published in the US press, a media campaign against UNESCO began. In a 1983 New York Times article, 'U.S. Is Quitting UNESCO, Affirms Backing For U.N.'[10] State Secretary of State George Schultz accused UNESCO that all this is just Soviet propaganda. According to him, UNESCO's actions have served anti-American political purposes for several years. The article claims that the administration of President Ronald Reagan is on the verge of tolerating the wrong policies of UNESCO. According to the US Government, these wrong UNESCO policies support Soviet disarmament proposals and collectivist trends and promote the group's rights at the expense of individual human rights. Also, UNESCO efforts to promote the licensing of foreign reporters and the creation of a New World Order Information. Special attention in the article is paid to the so-called new international economic order. It is assumed that rich countries will have to transfer resources to poorer ones. All this shows the direct link between the economic, communication, and information world order, in which Western countries have the upper hand. This fierce resistance and pressure from the West lead to a lasting end to the talks on the New Information Order in the international community. Because of a New Information Order request, the United States left UNESCO at the end of 1984, and Britain followed in 1986. In 1987 in Paris, after Amadou M'Bow of Senegal, Federico Mayor Zaragoza was elected Secretary-General from Spain. Thus, a New World Information Order discussion ends, and the idea is forgotten.

The lack of change in the power communication model ultimately leads to the monopolisation and unification of world culture. Infinite possibilities for different peoples to create new and new combinations of human ingenuity are lost. Instead, a global utilitarian culture tries to manufacture consent according to imposed cultural models and stereotypes. In this way, social creativity and progress are deliberately stopped. That is the warning of the MacBride Report about the transformation of individuals into passive audiences created by the ruling classes and their mass media. After 1980 the development of multinational media monopolies guarantees global information and communication dominance. There is a danger that the world will become a single media culture. A world in which we all try to look the same, think the same, and speak with the same stereotypes. Of course, this plan failed with the appearance of the Internet. The inherited freedom of the new technology created a global culture of dissent. Manufacturing consent was no longer possible. The old elites needed to adjust to the new era of chaotic and hostile communication.

Murdochisation

In the 21st century, the MacBride report and UNESCO's New World Information Order plan are mentioned only in academia. In the 2005 article 'From McBride to Murdoch: The Marketization of Global Communication'[11] Daya Kishan Thussu spoke of 'Murdoch's effect,' after media mogul Rupert Murdoch. The 'Murdochisation' of the media is related to the uneven distribution of information in the Third World. Global media's commercialization and market nature are obstacles to public media's educational and social functions. It is especially true in developing countries where education is not available to everyone. MacBride's report's concerns are still valid, even in the 21st century. On the Internet, the processes of liberalisation, deregulation, and privatisation mainly benefit transnational corporations, which dominate world trade and communication. 'Murdochisation' is an ideological change in world media culture. From service to society to the service of personal interests and disinformation for profit has adverse effects on the development of social creativity and leads to illiteracy and inequality. According to Daya Thussu, while Rupert Murdoch is the winner of the battle for the market model of the mass media, Sean McBride must be spinning in his grave. One of the characteristics of the market model of 'Murdochisation' of the media is the maintenance of high interest by the audience at all costs. An increased rating is guaranteed by producing disagreement between different groups in society. The goal is the division of the mass audience into hostile groups which have their media and channels of information. People will trust everything that supports their ideology as opposed to other groups. Thus, in the search for Internet traffic, media commercialization imposes a pattern of constant conflict and disagreement. However, there is little hope of resistance to the market model of online media. In 2015, The Federal Communications Commission voted on a document called 'Protecting and Promoting the Open Internet,' which defends net neutrality principles. In this document, FCC establishes rules for the protection and promotion of Open Internet Order. In particular, these rules prohibit blocking, 'bandwidth throttling,' and paid prioritisation of particular sources and content on the Internet. They prevent broadband providers from interfering unduly with communication between users. Greater equality and transparency in Internet management practices are ensured. In May 2017, however, FCC offers a new document, 'FCC Proposes Ending Utility-Style Regulation of The Internet First Step Toward Restoring Internet Freedom, Promoting Investment, Innovation & Choice.' It claims to restore freedom online and end the regulation on the Internet. This document will give massive power to ISPs to decide what content and what sources to allow. In practice, they will be able to perform censorship.

In a study from 2017 called 'Digital Planet 2017: How Competitiveness and Trust in Digital Economies Vary Across the World,'[12] the vast role of network neutrality in the development of the entire business ecosystem is emphasised. According to the study, the US digital economy is already on the verge of stagnation. The inability to defend the principle of an open internet will reduce the competitiveness of digital technologies and a lack of innovation. The Digital Evolution Index has also been developed, which determines the relative position of each country vis-à-vis others in the digital economy. Although these studies focus on the economic aspects of network neutrality, the germ of this idea can be traced to the theory of mass communication. The principle of neutrality of the carrier obliges it to refer to any product or information without prejudice or preferences and provides a favorable system for all equality of access to information. Communities and groups deprived of a level playing field and free supply of diverse information are more likely to stagnate and even disintegrate and divide. The very access to information and communication skills of individuals guarantee social development and raising social capital. These studies of the digital economy and the Internet confirm the conclusions of the MacBride Report on the importance of free and equal communication. The need to transform passive audiences into a real society, sharing a standard system of values and united around common goals. With the restriction of network neutrality, various regulation mechanisms of Internet media and social networks are being discussed more and more seriously. This regulation of news is somewhat contrary to the basic principles of freedom of speech. Over time any information published in the mass media can be fake or false. That is why every media outlet and journalist is responsible for publishing the truth. Freedom of speech laws is based on this trust in the media. Instead of censorship and labeling which news is 'real' and 'fake,' the media must follow their ethical codes. Unfortunately, these principles of independent journalism are once again in a foothold. It seems that all other mass media before and the Internet media will also lose their relative freedom. Every media gradually falls under the control of the state or business monopolies.

In the 21st century, the plan for the New Global Information Order of equality and agreement on the Internet turned out to be a total dystopia. It seems that every new communication model will be built on the principles of domination and power. However, the idea that better communication and free access to information lead to a better lifestyle is still alive today. The Internet allows for a link between researchers, journalists, the media, and audiences. It significantly reduces the possibility of elites' manipulation and social control, lobbies, and pressure groups. The academic community and communication researchers need to look for more adequate new models of mass communication. That can only be done through an atmosphere of spontaneous sharing and information equality.

1.4. Dysfunctions in the propaganda model

The term 'manufacturing consent,' made famous by the eponymous book[13] by Noam Chomsky and Edward Herman, was borrowed from American journalist and media researcher Walter Lippmann. One of the most-cited authors in the field of public opinion research for the 20th century, Lippmann, for the first time imposed the idea of 'manufacture of consent' as a global model of forming public opinion through mass media in democracies. This model aims to reach agreement and unity in the great society of the state. It uses all means of propaganda, censorship, and manipulation without violence and coercion. 'Manufacturing consent' is genuinely effective only among the audience of a single media system with common information channels. Before the Internet, official mass media completely took over the public space and became intermediaries of all social communication. Society exists as represented by the mass media. In a democracy, they have the task of 'manufacturing consent,' even when it does not exist.

The latent dysfunction of mass media

In his book from 1893, 'The Division of Labor in Society,' Emil Durkheim spoke about the social functions of the institutions. It distinguishes normal from pathological functioning, although the understanding of normality may be different for different cultures. Robert Merton continues this tradition and uses the functional method to study social institutions. It divides social functions and dysfunction into manifest and latent. The term 'latent dysfunction of communication' is close to the concepts of 'systematic distortion of communication' by Habermas and 'communication entropy' by Shannon and Weaver. The functional method makes it possible to detect these latent dysfunctions and understand the process of entropy in communication. The term 'entropy' in the exact sciences was used in 1865 by the German physicist Rudolf Clausius on the direction in which the change takes place in a material system. This change is always in the direction of disorder and energy dissipation, and entropy measures this chaos in the system. The second law of thermodynamics states that in a closed system, entropy can only increase. The system has maximum entropy when it is in thermodynamic equilibrium, which means that every closed system strives for chaos. In 1949, Claude Shannon and Claude Weaver introduced the term 'entropy in communication' and the concept of an amount of information in their 'Mathematical Theory of Communication.' Communication entropy is the level of predictability of information or the average amount of expected information in communication. The connection of entropy with the latent dysfunction of the system is that in the closed communication system, the entropy always increases. The amount of information decreases, communication is distorted, and the system becomes dysfunctional. The manufacturing of dissent, which leads to division into a communication system, is one of the manifestations of entropy—a form of communication chaos. While consent is the pursuit of order and maintenance of the system, disagreement creates a constant regime of destabilisation. It brings constant change and novelty and attracts attention. In the media universe, chaos pays. In 1990. Meryl, Lee, and Friedlander[14] view entropy as a negative trend in communication. It leads to a loss of information and efficiency. The question is if the goal of media is to deliver information and be efficient or instead to attract attention at any cost. The message may lose its information impact due to the intermediary in the communication or media. The moment the media chooses a message instead of another, the entropy process begins and continues with each new intervention. According to Meryl, Lee, and Friedlander, the entropy in mass communication cannot be avoided in every closed communication system. Disagreement in a closed communication system can only increase. An example of this is the totalitarian countries with state censorship of information. In such cases, the dissent may be temporarily suppressed by blowing steam in the temporary liberalisation of the censorship system. The only way to slow down entropy is for the communication system to be as open as possible to various messages and information. When the intervention of intermediaries is minimal, then stability lasts longer. Hope for such development of a communication system gives the Internet the possibility for the constant influx of new information. There is a technical possibility that the connection between the individuals is direct, without the need for media and intermediaries. The global Internet network has much lower entropy than all other mass communication systems due to the infinity of virtual space. An unlimited number of groups and communities can be created on the Internet. They enable all individuals who disagree with official public opinion to find others like them. These processes are potentially dangerous for the stability of any state system. Internet communities share information outside of state regulation and censorship. Thus, as the global network of Internet entropy slows down, the closed national system increases.

In 1936, American sociologist Robert Merton links entropy to the 'unintended consequences' and 'latent dysfunction' of the communication system. He spoke about the unforeseen consequences of purposeful social action in his eponymous article, 'The Unanticipated Consequences of Purposive Social Action.' The central paradox of social action is that realising values can lead to self-denial and abandonment. Merton is trying to apply systematic analysis to the problem of the unintended consequences of conscious actions aimed at causing social change. He warns that interventions in a complex system tend to create unexpected and often undesirable results. It is a warning to educated elites who are convinced that they can fully control the world around them. According to Merton, the possible causes of the unforeseen consequences include human stupidity, self-delusion, misunderstanding of human nature, and other cognitive or emotional deviations. One of these deviations is the increase of dissent in society and the loss of trust between different groups and individuals. In his book 'The Social Theory and Social Structure,' Merton introduced the concept of 'manifest and latent functions and dysfunctions' of communication. If negative results are expected from the apparent dysfunction, then latent dysfunction with unforeseen negative consequences is much more dangerous for the balance in the system. The revelation of latent functions and dysfunction in the communication of the sociocultural system makes it possible to understand the balance in society. This balance of interactions of its components is called functionality. The functional analysis examines the dynamics of latent functions and dysfunction to detect the cause of the imbalance. Merton points to the misconception that societies are, in principle, functional, and harmonious alliances. In them, people work well together, and everyone is well integrated. He gave an example of the black inhabitants of South Africa during Apartheid. An example of a case where societies are not necessarily functional for all people. It cannot be trusted that ideals work for everyone in society. Some things can be dysfunctional for some and functional for others. A functional communication system must strive to create feelings of consent and unity among all people, at least as far as possible. To determine whether positive functions exceed dysfunction (and vice versa), Merton develops the concept of the net balance. As this balance is based on a subjective judgment, it is impossible to simply sum up the positive functions and dysfunction and objectively determine which prevails over others. According to Merton, there must be levels of functional analysis, and an organisation, institution, or group should be analyzed instead of society as a whole. Merton's idea of 'Middle-range theories.' and the refusal of a grand theory for society leads to studies of specific communities at a particular time. Functional analysis is often declared a conservative and even reactionary method, the purpose of which is only to maintain the status quo. It is inevitable since communication itself in a nation-state has clearly defined functions, goals, and objectives. National unity and consent are often present as fundamental ideals enshrined in state constitutions. The pursuit of their preservation is a primary task for any government. When communication functions in society focus on certain ideals, functionalism means observing the general movement in the chosen direction. When media functions are not related to the 'public interest,' the media are given the power to determine this interest. That requires a straightforward critical approach to media activity.

Propaganda 2.0 online media model

Today, in many countries, society is presented on social networks on the Internet. Digital companies monopolise the worldviews of consumers. The profits of these companies are related to internet traffic, which is much higher in conflict. Online media is provoking moral anger systematically. The 'Angry people click more' model brings corporate profits and social decline in traditional societies. Walter Lippmann does not trust the wisdom of the crowds and their ability to build a reasonable and educated public opinion on their own. For him, the mass of people is a confused herd and cannot self-organise, nor can it draw up rational action plans. That is the task of a well-educated elite in the leadership of the mass media. This manipulation is needed in the name of the democratic process, but it must be based on a new theory of public opinion. Otherwise, public opinion becomes a tool for realising personal goals and private interests, leading to crises in democracy and dissent in society. Disagreement and dysfunction in public communication are the opposite effects of elite manipulation and democratic propaganda. Total manipulation of public opinion is impossible online. Free access to information and the ability to share any opinion is one of the great risks of liberal democracy. They lead to a crisis in the entire communication system of nation-states. Along with disinformation and fake news, the manufacture of dissent deserves the attention of media researchers as a serious public problem. The discovery and analysis of these dysfunctions in the democratic system today requires knowledge of their genealogy. There are theoretical and empirical indicators for their appearance in the study of mass media. One of the pioneers in studying communication dysfunction in a democratic society is Walter Lippmann. Lippmann's idea of the 'manufacture of consent' as a model of democratic propaganda was developed in his books 'Public Opinion' in 1922, 'The Phantom Public' in 1925, and 'The Public Philosophy' in 1955. In them, he warns of the limitations of democracy and the dangers for national states, which hide in government through free and uncontrolled public opinion. The search for and achievement of the 'consent of the governed' is a basic principle in political theory that legitimises the power of the rulers. In the name of this legitimacy, the media under the power elite's control must 'manufacture consent' instead of expecting it to arise independently. In the name of social unity, in liberal democracies, consent is produced by a media system related to state power. The media doesn't oppose state power. Media is the language of power. The danger comes in the absence of a single, educated elite to control the media. The lack of monopoly on information in the great society leads to division, disagreement, and chaos. Before World War II, democratic propaganda and the formation of public opinion became the main object of research in the United States. Two of the most famous names in this area are Edward Bernays and Harold Laswell. Edward Bernays developed Lippmann's ideas in his books 'Crystallizing Public Opinion' in 1923, 'Propaganda' in 1928, and 'The Engineering of Consent' from 1955. He openly affirms democratic propaganda as a basic communication model of democracy. Bernays believes in the need for 'engineering of consent' and indirectly occupies the term from Lippmann. Regarding the danger of revealing manipulation and propaganda by the audience, Bernays believes this is a useful process and will lead to a more educated and responsible audience. Research by American scientists has influenced the development of propaganda in Europe and especially in Germany. German propaganda minister Josef Goebbels is personally interested in the methods of American propaganda in peacetime. Before World War II, young German journalists and media researchers were sent to the United States. One of these specialists is the young journalist Elizabeth Noelle, who defended her doctoral dissertation at the University of Missouri in 1940. She then returned to Germany, where she worked briefly in the Nazi propaganda newspaper 'Das Reich.' Later, in 1974 Elizabeth Noelle-Neumann wrote an article published as a book in 1984, entitled 'The Spiral of Silence, Public Opinion—Our Social Skin.' In it, she explores the social nature of man and his innate conformism and readiness to accept the opinion of others. The fear of isolation is this spiral of silence that helps maintain cohesion and society. On the scale of nation-states, it is used for national purposes, propaganda, and social control. Thus, mass media can produce a public opinion with the power of general morality, relying on the consent of individuals who accept the majority's opinion. Noam Chomsky and Edward Herman call this system the 'Propaganda model of communication' in their book, 'Manufacturing Consent: The Political Economy of the Mass Media.' This model worked successfully in the western world after World War II until the end of the

20th century and the advent of the Internet. The propaganda model of communication is related to the idea of 'systematically distorted communication' by Jürgen Habermas. The distortion includes creating barriers to free communication for social control and domination. The influence of state and corporate interests on mass media and public communication is a key factor in this communication model. The media are losing their social function and becoming an ideological instrument of corporate propaganda. They try to manufacture consent only to maintain the status quo of power and dominance. All principles and myths of freedom of speech that the media promotes are just a cover for this purpose. At the beginning of the 21st century, the advent of the Internet began to destroy old propaganda myths and created a need for a new paradigm of communication. In 1992 Francis Fukuyama published his book 'The End of History and the Last Man,' where, along with the end of history, he declared the end of the ideologies as a way to create consent. The end of the story also means an end to faith in great ideas. The ideologies that guide society as a stable and passive group are now obsolete. Once history has exhausted its great promises for the future, it means the end of the masses who expect this future as a group. Fukuyama's 'last man' was the first man of the 21st century. He is an individualist who loses touch with the traditional community and creates a new network with other individuals. Social networks on the Internet put an end to the mass manufacturing of consent. The model is reversed, and individuals pursue personal and group goals in a new environment of mistrust and disagreement. Thus, traditional models of social control are the main dysfunction of public communication in a democratic society. They lead to tensions between groups and individuals in a new model of manufacture of dissent. The beginning of the Propaganda 2.0 model.

Notes

1 Mcquail, Denis. (2013). Reflections on paradigm change in communication theory and research. *International Journal of Communication*, 7, 216–229.
2 Burkart, R. (2002). *Kommunikationswissenschaft: Grundlagen und Problemfelder; Umrisse einer interdisziplinären Sozialwissenschaft.* Wien-Vienna: Böhlau.
3 Burkart, R. (2002). *Kommunikationswissenschaft: Grundlagen und Problemfelder; Umrisse einer interdisziplinären Sozialwissenschaft.* Wien-Vienna: Böhlau.
4 Mcquail, Denis. (2013). Reflections on paradigm change in communication theory and research. *International Journal of Communication*, 7, 216–229.
5 von Alemann, U. (1997). Parteien und Medien. In *Parteiendemokratie in deutschland*, pp. 478–494. Wiesbaden: VS Verlag für Sozialwissenschaften.
6 Postman, Neil. (1970). The reformed English curriculum. In *High school 1980: The shape of the future in American secondary education*. Edited by Alvin C. Eurich, 160–168. New York: Pitman.
7 McLuhan, Marshall. (1964). *Understanding media*. New York: Mentor.
8 Castells, M. (2010). *The power of identity, Volume 2, with a new preface*. Hoboken, NJ: Wiley-Blackwell.
9 The MacBride Report: Many Voices One World, UNESCO. http://unesdoc.unesco.org/images/0004/000400/040066eb.pdf (Last visited 16.06.2020).

10 "Gwertzman, Bernard. (30.12.1983). U.S. Iis Qquitting UNESCO, Aaffirms Bbacking Ffor U.N." By Bernard Gwertzman, *New York Times*. December 30, 1983.
11 Thussu, Daya Kishan. (2005). From Macbride to Murdoch: The marketisation of global communication. *Journal of the European Institute for Communication and Culture*, 12(3), 47–60.
12 The Fletcher School. (2017). *Tufts university, digital planet*. http://sites.tufts.edu/digitalplanet/dei17/ (Last visited 16.06.2020).
13 Chomsky, N., and E. S. Herman. (1994). *Manufacturing consent: The political economy of the mass media*. London: Vintage Books.
14 Merrill, John Calhoun, John Lee, and Edward Jay Friedlander. (1990). *Modern mass media*. New York: Harper & Row.

Reference list

1.1. The need for a new paradigm of communication

Burkart, R. (2002). *Kommunikationswissenschaft: Grundlagen und Problemfelder; Umrisse einer interdisziplinären Sozialwissenschaft*. Wien-Vienna: Böhlau.

Mcquail, Denis (2013). Reflections on paradigm change in communication theory and research. *International Journal of Communication*, 7, 216–229.

1.2. The rise of dissent in the network society

Castells, M. (2010). *The power of identity, Volume 2, with a new preface*. Hoboken, NJ: Wiley-Blackwell.

Castells, M., & C. Blackwell (1998). Volume 1: The information age: Economy, society, and culture: The rise of the network society. *Environment and Planning B: Planning and Design*, 25, 631–636.

McLuhan, Marshall (1964). *Understanding media*. New York: Mentor.

McLuhan, Marshall, & Eric McLuhan (1988). *Laws of media*. Toronto: University of Toronto Press.

Postman, Neil (1970). The reformed English curriculum. In *High school 1980: The shape of the future in American secondary education*. Edited by Alvin C. Eurich, pp. 160–168. New York: Pitman.

von Alemann, U. (1997). Parteien und Medien. In *Parteiendemokratie in Deutschland*, pp. 478–494. Wiesbaden: VS Verlag für Sozialwissenschaften.

1.3. The 'New World Information Order' utopia

The Fletcher School, Tufts University, Digital Planet (2017). http://sites.tufts.edu/digitalplanet/dei17/ (Last visited 16.06.2020).

Gwertzman, Bernard (December 30, 1983). The U.S. is quitting UNESCO, affirms backing for U.N. *New York Times*.

The MacBride Report: Many Voices One World, UNESCO. http://unesdoc.unesco.org/images/0004/000400/040066eb.pdf (Last visited 16.06.2020).

Thussu, Daya Kishan (2005). From Macbride to Murdoch: The marketisation of global communication. *Journal of the European Institute for Communication and Culture*, 12(3), 47–60.

www.fcc.gov/document/fcc-proposes-ending-utility-style-regulation-internet (Last visited 16.06.2020).
www.federalregister.gov/documents/2015/04/13/2015-07841/protecting-and-promoting-the-open-internet (Last visited 16.06.2020).

1.4. Dysfunctions in the Propaganda model

Herman, Edward S., & Noam Chomsky (2010). *Manufacturing consent: The political economy of the mass media*. Random House.

Merrill, John Calhoun, John Lee, & Edward Jay Friedlander (1990). *Modern mass media*. New York: Harper & Row.

Merton, Robert K. (1936). The unanticipated consequences of purposive social action. *American Sociological Review*, 1(6), 894–904.

Merton, Robert K. (1957). *Social theory and social structure, Rev.* New York: The Free Press.

Shannon, C. E., & W. Weaver (1949). *The mathematical theory of communication*. Urbana, IL: University of Illinois Press.

2 Dissent and the theory of mass communication

Peter Ayolov

This chapter presents eight general theories in mass communication and sociology, which directly link to the manufacture of dissent. The book tries to update the theories and find their significance in the Internet age concerning the dissent model. As the Internet gradually becomes the Fifth Estate, they appear more up-to-date and deserve a new reading. 21st-century media researchers can obtain a serious theoretical basis in the face of a clash with new phenomena. This further reading is related to the search for a new paradigm for communication in the tradition of Dennis Mcquail's ideas. All connections and reflections with the new media are a hypothesis and are subject to in-depth future research. However, fascinating coincidences with the observations on the influence of the media in the last century are found. It turns out that despite 21st-century digital technologies, the effects on society and individuals are very similar to the advent of electronic media in the 20th century. These theories give valuable guidance and hope for possible opposition to the systematic distortions of communication and the manufacture of dissent on the Internet. The eight theories are as follows: Walter Lippmann's 'Manufacture of Consent'; Edward Bernays' 'Democratic propaganda'; The 'Propaganda model' by Noam Chomsky; The 'End of History' by Francis Fukuyama; Elizabeth Noelle-Neumann's 'Spiral of Silence'; Maxwell McCombs' 'Agenda-Setting'; Nicklas Luhmann's 'System Theory of Pseudo-News'; and Jürgen Habermas' 'Systematic distortion of communication.'

2.1. 'Manufacture of consent'—Walter Lippmann

According to Walter Lippmann, the 'manufacture of consent' model is a kind of democratic propaganda or government public relations. Without such a system of information control and censorship, there is a danger in democracies of universal disagreement and division. Then democracy can degenerate into an oligarchy or dictatorship. On the other hand, the manufacture of dissent is the natural state of an unregulated communication system. As if on the principle of some social entropy, it constantly strives for chaos and division. The consent of the governed is always the result of an organised

DOI: 10.4324/9781003380207-3

plan and is seldom automatically generated. Consent between the governed is even more challenging. In every known state regime, order and understanding are achieved through systematic and purposeful communication regulation. Even in those in which censorship is prohibited by law. Thus, mass media became the main stage of political processes. Media content determines political discourse in the nation-state. Forming public opinion is the first task of democratic governance. This process must be monitored to avoid dysfunctions in the communication system. Imposing a chaotic model of dissent, in which the media gain enormous power, is a danger to democracy. The purpose of most mass media theories is to impose order in the chaos of dissent. Therefore, theoretical indicators for this pattern of dissent can be found in many authors and researchers of 20th-century mass communication. First on this list is the name, Walter Lippmann. In his 1920 book called 'Liberty and News,'[1] Lippmann asks whether national unity in democracy is possible. How to reach an agreement in the presence of freedom of speech and with so many differences between people? How can there be a single public opinion when every citizen can opinion on all critical issues and express it publicly? Lippmann answers that unity and peace are possible only between informed people who seek the unity of method rather than of aim. These people use the scientific method and experiments to study the environment. They have an educated opinion about the events around them, and in this social environment, the contradictions between them are creative. Dissent is a child, not of different opinions, but the un-education of individuals. The problem is the lack of a scientific method that checks the facts and seeks the truth. Lippmann believes in the possibility of creating an educated public opinion and at the same time warns of the dangers that may arise along the way. For him, democracy is not a given or a stable thing. On the contrary, an impermanent state requires constant effort from an educated community. Democracy can be lost at any time. Lippmann emphasised the need for regulation and rules for mass communication and information processes in his first works. For him, the modern understanding of free man means freedom for the educated and knowledgeable man. Only through the scientific method, analysis, and access to the sources of information can one feel free and form an opinion. This educated opinion is not an end in itself or a means of self-expression. Its purpose is not a dispute or competition with other opinions. The goal is to influence others. To manufacture consent without which there can be no society at all. According to Lippmann, the real enemy is ignorance, and democracy is not possible among ignorant people. Above all, it is a contract between beliefs and realities. The ability of people to educate themselves is the opportunity to connect with reality. Education is the guarantee of a democratic society. When people trust the competition of opinions in the media, it leads to misery and confusion. There is also a danger that democracy will degenerate into a dictatorship. Democracy will survive if it reaches an agreement and self-government. Creating a direct link between beliefs and realities is the utopia of the lost democracy of the small town.

In times of peace and security, public opinion leaders are subject to constant scrutiny and are challenged by society. These images are placed under surveillance in long periods of calm and begin to crack. Lack of leadership leads to instability and dissent in every group of people. The only way to restore faith in these symbolic personalities is to threaten an external enemy and destruction. For Lippmann, there is only one human activity where all people achieve an absolute union: war. Public opinion leaders are born heroically in the war of ideas, dissent, and conflict. Then comes a truce, and administrators gradually replace the characters. The moment people realise that great personalities are just administrators, the system needs recharging. The communication system needs times of dissent to recharge itself. A new period of clashes, wars of opinion, division, and disagreement follows. And so on to a new war or a big crisis of all kinds.

The 'pseudo-environment' of democracy

In his book 'Public Opinion,' Lippmann seeks the genesis of public opinion in a constant cycle of war and peace. A cycle of alternation of consent and dissent. Unlike authoritarian regimes and dictatorships, democracy is a continuous clash of opinions and systematically produces dissent. As the actual environment is too complex for direct knowledge, a good democratic government must reconstruct it at a simplified conditional level. Public opinion is a fabrication, a conditional geographical map on which one is guided in the world. The lies that describe the world are only a way to present the environment, and the result of fiction can have almost any degree of credibility. It is natural for a man to lie and invent because he narrates himself. His function in society is much more important than his understanding of reality. Proximity to facts and truth has no social value. The truth is only this idea of the reality that works in a public system. Regardless of the degree of authenticity, other people's truth is always a lie and a fabrication. Hostile propaganda can create conditions for total ideological wars of the destruction of the enemy. Lippmann describes them as two armies fighting to the death; each of them is convinced that they are acting in self-defense. During such a war, the two peoples were ready to destroy themselves, each with the conviction that his victory would be in the interest of all humanity. Thus, society becomes united in the name of the promised common good. The unity of society is achieved in a 'pseudo-environment' that determines thought, feeling, and action. People create pseudo-images of distant and close worlds through language, stories, drawings, books, newspapers, radio, and television. In the public sphere, these world images value absolute truth about reality. Unity in a group of people has achieved the fastest through the 'manufacture of consent' based on some threat, some common enemy. The problem with the pseudo-environment is not just a communication problem. It underpins the successful functioning of a democratic state. The masked flaw of democracy is that citizens cannot be competent in all cases or informed on all topics. An omission that has yet to be taken. Understanding the media as a panacea for the shortcomings of democracy only hinders its favorable functions. Above all, media create a space for communication that produces consent and unity in society. If access to the natural environment and the facts are open, creating a pseudo-environment is impossible. Free access to the facts always creates the danger of disagreement and division. In cases where this access is given, mechanisms are always put in place to divert the audience's attention from the natural environment through a series of sensational and extreme pseudo-events. In extreme cases, even with directed military action. According to Lippmann, democratic propaganda is not possible without censorship. You make sure that before creating a pseudo-environment, you must restrict access to the real world.

Military propaganda and preparation for war act not only as a test of the unity of the state but also as a test of the very reality in which its citizens live. During a war, all pseudo-environments disappear and are replaced by the world of survival. War is an undemocratic human activity if democracy means pluralism and freedom of opinion. It requires a clear hierarchy and distribution of power. During a war, the need to impose a single opinion stands out. Dissent is more dangerous than lies and fabricated consent. Two opposing views are more hazardous than a misconception; even one of them is true. One wrong opinion may lead to bad consequences, but the two opinions together can lead to a whole disaster if, thanks to them, unity falls apart. One bad general is better than two good ones.

Manufacture of consent in the mass media

Propaganda during war works so successfully that it is always tempting to use it in peacetime. The military threat, whether inside or outside, allows for totalitarian rule. Interestingly, this is happening in a democratic environment and on behalf of the people. When it is impossible to justify an aggressive war with an external enemy, conflicts within society serve as a form of social control. During two wars, propaganda created a climate of disagreement and tension through a war of opinions. Public opinion leaders assert their public authority in a constant state of dissent. For them, continuing their command is such a sacred goal that it can justify all the means used. The manufacture of consent in a community of people is the primary goal of every statesman and politician. If he reaches this agreement, he naturally becomes a leader in public opinion and wins the group's trust. Regardless of the real consequences of his actions, he will always be judged mainly by his public image. The leaders of public opinion highly value the group's unity. Consent is much more important than truth or prosperity and material gains. Great politicians are always leaders of public opinion and unifiers of the nation. The very public image of these figures becomes a national symbol and produces consent. The manufacture of consent in human communities in the 20th century is slowly becoming a perfect tool for social control. As Lippmann notices, this is something more important even than economic development:

'The creation of consent is not a new art. It is a very old one that was supposed to have died out with the appearance of democracy. But it has not died out. It has improved enormously in technic because it is now based on analysis rather than the rule of thumb. And so, as a result of psychological research, coupled with the modern means of communication, the practice of democracy has turned a corner. A revolution is taking place, infinitely more significant than any shifting of economic power.'[2]

Public opinion and the risk to democracy

The main advantage of democracy is to find unity in the difference. It can quell tensions and create consent through mass manipulation and propaganda. In the 21st century, enmity and disagreement between different groups became the biggest challenge for democracy. The ultimate form of this hostility in democracies is armed conflicts and attempts to return to authoritarian regimes. The power of propaganda in mass society questions the faith in democracy. At the heart of democracy is the ideal for protecting the freedom and the right to vote of every person in society. It is done through representative chosen ones who protect the rights of specific people. The communication between voters and electives is at the heart of democratic ideology. The elected representative expresses the public opinion of his community before the general meeting. Thus, the opinion of every citizen finds its representation and can be formally stated and discussed. Democrats are always primarily interested in events within the community and defend the existence of a pseudo-environment. In it, members of the community find meaning. Within this closed community, the manufacture of consent is a primary task, but the opposite principle works outside it. Outside the community, conflict is sought, and dissent with other communities is 'manufactured.' It is also called conflict propaganda. This external disagreement strengthens internal unity. Democracies are never very strong in external diplomacy because of the higher law of the people's voice. Lippmann notes that any form of government other than democracy is a threat and is seen as a declaration of war. Democrats are convinced that any contact with the world outside the pseudo-environment poses a threat to democracy. This belief in the perfection of democracy leads to a lack of interest in citizens in the political system. The result is a lack of control over the government. Ultimately the result is inequality and dissent. War is the only political act that re-creates a community of opinions and consolidates society. The desire to unite public opinion leads to democratic wars and conflicts as a means of social control. For Lippmann, democratic wars broke out because of pacifist goals, and this is something new in human history. They are believed to be guided in the name of all human civilization. Crises of democracy lead to total wars in the name of the complete victory of democracy worldwide.

These wars begin with propaganda. Every democratic state officially devotes efforts and resources to promoting its values and ideology. In 1922 Walter Lippmann pessimistically reminded us of a possible World War II danger. The manufacture of dissent between states is the only way to trump internal dissent. Lippmann's paradox is that the more people have personal freedom, the more conflicts, and disagreements. He hopes that all these struggling groups with different opinions and incompatible pseudo-environments can listen to the voice of reason and exist in parallel. Maybe the future of democracy lies in a Metaverse of parallel pseudo-environments.

2.2. 'Democratic propaganda'—Edward Bernays

Edward Bernays is considered the father of public relations (PR) and the creator of the profession of the Public Relations Council. He introduced the term PR in the theory of communication and sociology. Bernays develops Walter Lippmann's ideas on the need for an educated elite and propaganda in democracies. The elite must lead the masses and manipulate public opinion in the name of manufacturing consent and unity in society. This intelligent minority of specialists must even create news. It may direct pseudo-events in the name of consent. Today, because of the need to study the phenomenon of fake news on the Internet, Bernays' ideas are again of interest.

Public opinion and public relations

After 1920 and the Peace Conference in Paris, interest in public opinion increased, and the word propaganda began to be used everywhere. The remarkable effectiveness of propaganda during the war shows the possibility of using the same publicity practices in peacetime. The term 'public opinion' entered the Webster Dictionary in 1919. In 1923 Bernays' book 'Crystallizing Public opinion'[3] was published. The same year with his help, New York University established its first university course in public relations. Bernays notes that the great poverty, misery, and social inequality during the Great Depression led millions of Americans to be much more interested in the political and social structure. Every critical decision and power action must be coordinated with public opinion. Bernays gives concrete examples of the benefits of the new profession of public relations counsel, but above all, he is interested in public relations with the forces that create it. He takes as a starting point the motto of the New York Times: 'All the news that's fit to print.' But who decides which news is suitable for printing? What is the criterion for determining which news is fit? The lack of a common criterion makes it challenging to create an open space for ideas, similar to the ancient Greek agora. An opportunity is created for manipulation and control over the free exchange of views and opinions. According to Bernays, news fit for publication meets the approval of enough people, which allows the newspaper to exist. It is only natural for editors and media owners to be interested first in the interests of the media instead of those of society. Specific questions arise if the appropriate news reflects the relationship between individuals, organisations, and the state. Who regulates this process? Who decides what is essential and good for the nation? Who cares for the appropriate news to form a unified public opinion on important issues? How does the news participate in the manufacturing model of national consent and unity? In the first place in society, an agreement must be reached on the criteria for choosing news. The media must then strive for these standards. Otherwise, the media will be guided only by the pursuit of excellent circulation and profit. No matter how hard they try to form public opinion on crucial issues, they often follow it. The media began to follow the crowd, and it is difficult to say if the audience runs the institutions or the institutions run the public. The chaos of dissent is created when the media starts to publish only in the name of their interests.

The functions of the mass media

The issue of morality in the media is at the heart of the difference between propaganda and education. For Bernays, the only difference between them is their point of view. The advocacy of what you believe is education and advocacy for what you do not think is propaganda. The task of power in nation-states is to agree with many people with different interests and opinions. According to Bernays, society cannot wait until the absolute truth is found, and it must fabricate a working truth that creates consent. We can call it an abstract truth (so-called truth) substitute for the unattainable absolute truth. In the name of consent, society uses the so-called truths born of compromises between the desires and opinions of millions of individuals. It is essential for the new ideas to become significant through their acceptance by the group. That is why society is always in a real battle of ideas. The entire development of humanity, especially social progress, depends on how public opinion is formed. The future of this formation is the future of civilization. Its power will continue to grow and be enhanced by impulses from below, posing a direct danger to human society's progressive development and spiritual upliftment. Bernays is convinced that the duty of the higher strata of society, or the educated, knowledgeable, experts, and intellectuals, is to inject moral and spiritual motives into public opinion. Public opinion must become a public conscience. The nation's public conscience is the highest criterion that should regulate the choice of news and the creation of events. The formation of public opinion is carried out only in the name of consent and unity in the great society of the nation-state. Edward Bernays warns that if these persuasive influence techniques are used for personal and group purposes, the result is a division into society and a loss of trust between people.

The need for democratic propaganda

In 1928, Edward Bernays wrote the book 'Propaganda'[4] to clear the name of this ancient social control technique from the negatives accumulated during the First World War. He talks about new propaganda that underpins democracy and can be used in all spheres of life. Its goal is to organise chaos and create a social order built on a common consensus. In the name of this goal, conscious and intelligent manipulation of organised habits and opinions of the masses in a democratic society is performed. Bernays sees this new government and acknowledges how those who manipulate this invisible mechanism of society constitute a secret government that holds the real power to govern the country. The majority is aware of this manipulation, but it gives its tacit consent to it in the name of public order. Power in democracy is based on conscious and intelligent manipulation of organised habits. This process must be cleverly concealed so as not to provoke dissent. In this way, many human beings can cooperate and live together as a functioning society. Without propaganda and manipulation, it is impossible to manufacture consent between so many people living in one place. The social nature of man dominates the individual pursuit of knowledge and freedom. Public opinion is the delusion that millions of people think the same way. Without this delusion, the state cannot exist. Bernays does not trust in raising the universal literacy of the ordinary person. Just because he can read and write doesn't mean that he can govern. Despite the rise of education and literacy, the claim of the democratic doctrine of the collective mind has no practical evidence. For Bernays, the collective reason is born in communication and relationships between individuals and groups, not created through education. Education is a form of propaganda, and only in free contact with other people can one gain actual knowledge. Universal literacy is mass production that creates only stereotypes. The language became only a vessel for advertising slogans, editors' opinions, polls, trivial gossip from the tabloids, and banalities of history. Literacy is just a cliché that is far from the original thought. The American public receives more of its ideas at a fashion sale of ideas called propaganda. The incredible success of propaganda before and during the First World War opened the eyes of a small group of intelligent people to the opportunities to organise and control the public mind in peacetime. The US government explored this new technique, and Bernays was one of the first researchers. He simply describes the transition from managing leaders who do whatever they want to the management of rulers. The rulers must seek the approval of public opinion for each of their actions and, accordingly, cannot do anything without the help of propaganda. It is the language of power, but it uses the manufacture of consent instead of commands. The new network power uses persuasion instead of coercion. It thrives by the approval of the masses. For Bernays, propaganda is here to stay.

Why should public opinion be manipulated?

Bernays believes in the power of a group to convince a great society of his opinion. He describes the methods for this in his 1928 article with the eloquent title 'Manipulating Public Opinion: The Why and The How.'[5] He sees public opinion as the mind of society, but only at one determined moment and on a specific topic. This opinion is not a sum of all group opinions, nor is it something organic whole obtained in their interaction. Traditions and mass habits have a significant impact on public opinion. Bernays calls them the inertia of society. This constant repetition of habits and beliefs is the cumulative retrograde force of inertia, limiting civilization's development. The manipulator's task should not be selfish but protect society from possible aggression. Manipulation of public opinion must change when it is too conservative. Manipulation aims to disrupt public inertia when it is retrograde. Then we need a violent change in public opinion as a way for society to enter new ideas. Manipulation of public opinion must monitor and eliminate taboos and prejudices that hinder progress. For Bernays, public opinion is the power of an organised and cohesive group of people to swing a large audience to specific ideas. Public opinion is generally slow and reactionary, and difficult to accept new ideas. Progress requires mass production and distribution of industrial products and thoughts and opinions. The technique of forming public opinion among vast masses of people is part of this social and individual progress. Innovators are developing a new technology of mass persuasion, through which they have the power to change public opinion. Thus, the manipulation of public consciousness has a social goal or the audience's acceptance of new beliefs and habits.

The engineering of consent

In 1947, Bernays wrote an essay which in 1955 grew into a book called 'The Engineering of Consent.' Unlike the term 'manufacture of consent' by Walter Lippmann, he uses the word 'engineering,' but with the same meaning. The engineering of consent means that it cannot simply be suggested. Consent must be planned and developed through a mass technique for manipulation and forming public opinion. But is this manipulation morally justified? When freedom of speech and media independence is guaranteed in a liberal society, the right to influence is also guaranteed with persuasion, manipulation, and propaganda. For Bernays, freedom of speech and free press also includes freedom of persuasion and manipulation. Today with the further development of media technology, the doors to the public mind are opened. Everyone is equally free to attempt to control the moods and opinions of others. Bernays is aware of the dangerous power of propaganda, whose techniques he has developed and practiced all his life. However, he cannot foresee the consequences when this power is available. The revolution of communication technologies has led to an incredible exchange of ideas in which words became commands and slogans. Everyone has the freedom to influence the opinion of others online. Corporate media and individuals' social networks have an advantage over official national media in this network. No intelligent and educated elite must form public opinion in the name of the common good. It has been replaced by anyone who wins the public battle for popularity and attention. Bernays warns of creating a network of intertwined, repetitive, and mixed channels like the Internet. This network gives great strength to anyone who understands its action and the principles of creating consent in society. Like any technology, it is neutral and depends on the people who use it. We reject the authoritarian discipline commands, but we are open to being influenced and manipulated by words. For Bernays, democracy is impossible without manipulation and propaganda, as well as without the ability of leaders to use their methods. These are the unwritten rules of democracy, which are necessary for its existence. The lack of organised national propaganda leads to a vacuum filled by propaganda campaigns with personal and group interests. The other danger in the absence of national propaganda is foreign propaganda, which harms the unity of the state. National consent must be 'engineered' through a rational plan by trained people who believe in the national ideal. Only then will the ideas invested in words become part of the people they target. Communication is the key to creating consent as social action. Communication in this sense means not only the transmission of information but the knowledge of the people to whom this information is transmitted and the creation of a connection between them. Shared information becomes a social bond and a common experience. Thus, manipulation becomes a commitment process, and the manipulators become dependent on the community they manipulate. For Bernays, engineering consent is not just a marketing strategy for businesses but an effective social strategy for creating and maintaining human communities. The lack of such an organised system leads to dissent, clashes between different opinions, and the division of society into hostile groups. Whether in the traditions of a democratic state or on social networks of the Internet, consent in a group does not happen simply by itself. According to Bernays, consent is produced only through one rational and purposeful plan. Consent and trust are the highest ideals of the human community, and their creation and maintenance are the main task of democracy.

2.3. 'The spiral of silence'—Elizabeth Noelle-Neumann

Elizabeth Noelle-Neumann's book 'The Spiral of Silence, Public Opinion—Our Social Shell'[6] was published for the first time in 1980. It presented a new perspective on public opinion and questioned the basic postulates of democratic theory. Noelle-Neumann doubts the wisdom of the collective mind and sees it as a collection of selfish aspirations for belonging to the community. Individuals seek consent only for fear of isolation and the pursuit of recognition in society. The lack of this fear of isolation triggers the manufacture of dissent, which ultimately leads to disintegration. In the foreword to the 2001 book, Noelle-Neumann again defends his hypothesis about the 'spiral of silence.' This model of human social nature is to be studied in detail in the new 21st century. According to her, there is a real danger to human society, which is guided by people with misconceptions about the social nature of man. The very existence of society is a mystery.

Not understanding people's behavior can easily lead to disintegration, no matter how big the group is and its traditions. This fragmentation may not be physical but simply a loss of general morality or general opinion that has a soldering and regulating function. Human society is something alive and dynamic, and in the absence of communication, it simply becomes a network of individuals living together. Such a group of people is no longer a society because it is not united by common morality. Each member is free to leave the group without risking isolation. That is the threat of the manufacturing dissent model, which is imposed through the Internet and social networks.

Public opinion as a social bond

The main idea of the spiral of silence is that the individual always complies with public opinion to demonstrate belonging to a group. The individual's group interest is above the personal, and the social nature of man prevails. Even when people see clearly that a road is wrong, they prefer to remain silent. They avoid speaking the truth because they can isolate themselves. Agreement in society is a constant compromise between personal and public conscience. That compromise is a daily activity, as a constant weight and tension for the individual. He must judge his every opinion, according to the opinion of others. Freedom to disagree is always dangerous for traditional communities. The moment the spiral of silence stops working, the connections in society weaken. If they want to maintain their relative freedom and equality, individuals are forced to endure the yoke of the majority. Preserving public morality means a sign of obedience. Based on unwritten laws, this morality is not fixed. Its basic principle is the full power of the majority in the name of consent and unity. Public morality puts society above the individual. He needs to adjust to the others and start singing in tune. For Noelle-Neumann, the function of public opinion is in its publicity itself. The aim is not to share individual opinions at all costs but to create a climate of opinion that supports the dominant view. Public opinion is only an occasion to create a community and acts as a public bond. It does not solve a problem and simply demonstrates unity and agreement on the subject.

Social control

Each cohesive group of people is guided by the principle of the spiral of silence. Anyone who expresses a different opinion from the group risks getting into a negative attitude and isolation. Even the violation of legal laws is not such a serious crime in the eyes of society. Apparent disagreement with unwritten social norms leads to isolation. People can avoid prosecution, but no one can avert public 'denial and disapproval.' The communication theory also reflects this understanding of the need for control and opinion formation. According to Noelle-Neumann, with the advent of the 20th century, the concept of public opinion disintegrated, and the concept of social control was imposed. The new power is aware of public opinion and the power of the crowds. Masses of people need to be guided and guided in a new way. The rise of propaganda and manipulation in state governance is related to the development of technologies for mass communication, such as cinema and radio. At that time, the obsession with studying public opinion from political science and sociology became a more order of political parties. At the beginning of the 20th century, polls began to be conducted in the United States over the presidential election. Usually, in pursuit of higher circulation, the newspapers are the initiators. The very publication of the research itself becomes news. Thus, public opinion can be a prosecutor, a jury, and a judge in public affairs. Compared to the justice system, it is flexible, fast, and cheap. Official science abandoned the study of public opinion as instinctive and repetitive as part of man's social nature. Public opinion and sociological research are becoming tools for influence from power and business. Thus, the conscious management of opinion is established. Social control is based on the fear of isolation of the individual and his inability to live so as not to be influenced by the beliefs and opinions of others.

The end of public opinion

At the beginning of the 21st century, the number of people who openly declared themselves against public morality and destroyed moral consensus increased. On the one hand, the opportunity to participate in and leave different communities gives the individual unprecedented freedom and courage. On the other hand, public pressure is growing online. The virtual neighbors on the Internet are constantly monitored. Individuals do not feel fear of isolation and know that they can always find other online friends. Discovering other individuals close to your opinion on every issue is lightning fast. This social creativity of the Internet not only transcends geographical and state borders. Virtual communities transcend culture, ethnicity, race, ideology, religion, and even language boundaries. The Internet becomes a fundamental social reality in which individuals form an identity. It seems that in online communities, the bondage of public opinion has finally been rejected. It is as if the spiral of silence is destroyed, and one is free to live without fear of isolation. However, this new freedom inevitably leads to the manufacture of dissent within the traditional social structures of the nation-state. Public division can even begin with something insignificant at first glance, for example, music, fashion, and youth subcultures. For a large society, unwritten norms are equally crucial as official laws. If these norms lose their moral basis, then they are not observed. Changing fashion or music can lead to the disintegration of the community. If public opinion does not regulate the relationship between people, their relationship is falling apart. Society exists only by historical inertia, without a moral consensus among individuals. In this crisis of public morality, all power loses its legitimacy. The individual no longer feels moral obligations to observe the norms of society and the laws of the state.

Unwritten consent laws

The human community maintains the agreement between individuals and their integrity thanks to the personal feelings of each individual. This meaning is contained in the English word for 'consent,' which means 'manufacture of consent.' The meaning of 'consent' is from the Latin 'consentire,' which means 'to feel together.' Accordingly, 'dissent' implies the absence of that general feeling. When groups of individuals in a nation disagree on basic moral principles, it threatens its integrity. The challenge for a modern state is to continue to create consent among all despite the coexistence of groups with different social morals. In this process, education and propaganda are two stages in creating consent. The consent sought is not so much a rational consensus as a general sense of cohesion and togetherness. Both education and propaganda aim for all individuals to feel part of something in common. The media's main objective is not the search for truth but the imposition of a unified social morality. Noelle-Neumann asks the question of the paradox between the degree of individual independence and the cohesion of society. To what extent and how can a person resist and isolate from society, and what are the social effects? How independent can a person be? This question is related to the essence of human nature and its innate conformism. The word 'conformism' contains the meaning of unity and togetherness, not just consent and obedience. The word 'conform' comes from the Latin 'together' (com) and 'formare.' The Latin word 'conformare' (to fashion, to form, to shape) makes sense of 'education, formation, and modification,' according to fashion or public opinion. According to Noelle-Neumann, conformism and the spiral of silence are the basis of the social nature of the individual. Above all, to be human, he must demonstrate his ability to live in a community with other people. Dissent and personal independence have value only for the individual expressed in a community.

According to Noelle-Neumann, every society has the right to use the threat of isolation as a means of social control. But liberal democracy faces a crisis when censoring all anti-democratic views. Internet and the creation of new communities create some new crowds among which any opinion is admissible. Public morality in traditional societies has the power to isolate deviant individuals. Public opinion is our social shell, and individuals are victims because it is an enemy of the individual and a defender of society. For Noelle-Neumann, public opinion is a necessary evil for the individual and a basis for human civilization. This understanding is also at the heart of any political system. The bitter truth is that individuals rarely act as a collective without any coercion or manipulation. The mechanisms of the spiral of silence and the manufacture of consent can create a single society without the need for violence. It seems that these principles still work well online.

2.4. 'The propaganda model'—Noam Chomsky and Edward Herman

In 1988, Noam Chomsky and Edward Herman exposed the manipulative techniques for social control through the mass media in their book 'Manufacturing Consent: The Political Economy of the Mass Media.' The present book is a humble attempt to follow similar tendencies in the realm of the Internet. Chomsky and Herman's ideas are opposite to those of Lippmann and Bernays, and manufacturing consent is negative. Chomsky and Herman believe in the possibility of creating consent through open and equal dialogue in an influential media system. According to them, the propaganda model of mass media undermines the foundations of democratic ideology.

Media under control

In his article, 'Media Control: The Spectacular Achievements of Propaganda' from 1991, Chomsky described American democracy as 'spectators democracy.' He asks the question of the role of the media in a democratic society.

> 'The issue is whether we want to live in a free society or whether we want to live under what amounts to a form of self-imposed totalitarianism, with the bewildered herd marginalised, directed elsewhere, terrified, screaming patriotic slogans, fearing for their lives, and admiring with awe the leader who saved them from destruction, while the educated masses goose-step on command and repeat the slogans they're supposed to repeat, and the society deteriorates at home.'[7]

The question of the bewildered herd still awaits its answer. Whether the audience has the strength, skills, and ability to actively create independent and free public opinion and participate in state affairs? In the other case, it must accept the guidance and control of the elite. The manufacture of consent through the media became an open process, and the servitude is self-imposed. Chomsky disagrees with Lippmann and Bernays on the need for democratic propaganda. Democracy does not need a special class of intelligent people but a mass education. All citizens in a democracy must be educated, responsible, and smart. According to Chomsky, warring ideologies are united by the principle of power. Despite their claims, they do not intend to follow the people's interests. They have had this opportunity many times, but it is not in their interest. The question of strength rules the political machine, which is set according to the wishes of the elites or the crowds. Public dialogue is always a bargain for the consent of the governed, a dialogue between those who have power and property and those who do not. This problem of democracy has a possible solution in small groups and local communities. Only there is an opportunity for direct control of the members of any parliament at any time.

Properly functioning democracy

Chomsky expressed doubts about Lippmann's ideas of a gradual democracy in which the educated elite guided the confused herd. At some point, the public must become trained enough to be organised independently. Chomsky asks the question of what properly functioning democracy means. It should be a dominant goal in the development of social governance. Democracy is always a process and development instead of a complete and self-sufficient model—a process toward the growing participation of most people in the country. Chomsky describes the Propaganda model for manufacturing consent as a permanent model for social control. But once the shortcomings of a government from a single special class have been described, the democratisation of the public process is needed. Still, it does not happen because the real power is in those who control forming public opinion. However, a bewildered herd can never be tamed entirely, and the dissident wave in the 1960s shows it. A crisis of democracy starts when large parts of the population begin to become more active and organised. Unrepresented groups are trying to take part in political life. The dissatisfaction and dissent with the government become a constant state. Modern democracy can no longer exist without informal and hidden propaganda and censorship of the mass media. At the same time, no democratic state can openly acknowledge its existence. The need for manufacturing consent and crowd control cannot be discussed openly, at least as Lippmann did in the early 20th century. No one can afford to openly call the audience a 'bewildered herd' in the Internet age. It is not customary to speak openly about propaganda, censorship, media bias, and manipulation of democracy. The other media tabu is media and power relations. The propaganda model in democracy does a better job than violence in dictatorships. Everything changed with the advent of online media and social networks. As good as the methods of state propaganda are, they no longer affect the majority of the population. The distrust of official media reports is high. Today, propaganda works only to consolidate and radicalise an opinion. It has long been a technique for suggesting and changing opinions. People are increasingly starting to use information from the mass media with the awareness that it is part of some propaganda strategy. The audience agrees to participate in the game, supporting one of its chosen countries in advance. Propaganda in the media is recognisable and automatically creates dissent that leads to the opposition of hostile groups in society. The dissent and the constant conflict attract huge audiences in the new digital media and social networks.

The propaganda model in the 21st century

In the 21st century, many people in developed democracies are much more informed and conscious of the processes of propaganda and manipulation. The propaganda model does not work well, and instead of consent, it begins to produce growing dissent. However, people consciously accept an ideological position to defend regardless of truth and scientific facts. The Internet is creating a new virtual crowd that is no longer the typical mass of people who receive information from controlled channels. In this network of individuals and groups, everyone becomes a conductor of various propaganda. The goal is to unite the group by creating a threat and pointing to the enemy. The online propaganda model violates consent precisely because of multiple-choice propaganda narratives. The lack of censorship and official national propaganda leads to a constant war of ideas in the media of all democracies. Propaganda must be seen mainly as an intention. It is an organised communication strategy for a purpose. The goal of propaganda is always to achieve unity and consent in a particular community, often by pointing out an enemy. Sometimes this is at the expense of conflict with another community which is increasingly difficult between nations. So instead of consent, the propaganda model produces disagreement and tension within the nation. The new online propaganda is increasingly becoming a tool for protecting group and corporate interests from the state's priority. The most effective propaganda has counter-propaganda against it and is in constant competition. Propaganda 2.0 and the manufacture of dissent do not always have political goals and often follow purely commercial logic. Consumer culture is increasingly becoming a well-resolved reality and beginning to impose its principles in all spheres of social life. New virtual communities are being created and manipulated to sell more goods, not serve the public sphere. On the Internet, voters' views became consumers' views. Media business imposes a culture of entertainment that erodes the public sphere. Almost all media became commercial media. Political apathy followed, and politics became a television show. People are increasingly connected through their goods, services, tastes, and opinions than political beliefs. Goods and brands become communication objects, connecting people through their attitudes. Simultaneously with the goal of selling goods, entertainment is a channel for ideological messages that divert attention from politics. For Chomsky, political apathy helps maintain the status quo. But in the realm of social networks and the Internet, the apathy became moral anger, and the spectators became a herd of wild individuals. Consent is no longer possible.

At the beginning of the 21st century, the Internet and digital media became prominent globally and faced various interests. Once the media is part of the global economic system, they are also influenced by the changes that are taking place in the worldwide economy. National media systems are gradually losing power, and it is much harder to find hidden propaganda systems in private media. Official censorship is absent, and self-imposed political correctness is in use. It's a trade with information, communication channels, discussion spaces, and virtual communities. There is a clash with the old traditional systems of economic power. The new digital elites of the communication business impose new management ideas that conflict with the old ones. Internet media are exempt from control by nation-states.

They impose ideas that protect the interests of new international elites. The propaganda model gradually shifts to a market model of the media, and the dissent is marginalised and used as a commodity. Anger, dissent, and conflict draw people to specific topics and certain virtual spaces. The propaganda model in the 21st century reflects the clash between new types of power in a networked society. The network power results from the standards required to coordinate social network interaction. It affects all groups of the interests and choices of the mass media. Network power manages to filter the news that is fit for publishing but only in the pseudo-environment of inevitable digital media bubbles. Dissent is marginalised inside the groups, and dominant private interests deliver their messages to the public.

The necessary illusions

In the propaganda model of the 20th century, the media served public purposes but were under the control of an educated elite who decided on behalf of society. During the Cold War, consent was produced by uniting against the external enemy. In the 21st century, this model continues to work but no longer has a connection to the public interest. The manipulation of public opinion is in the name of the economic, social, and political interests of privileged groups that dominate society and the state. Digital media is owned by commercial corporations whose main product is their audiences. The people and their stories and interactions are the primary commodities of this business model. Internet traffic increases if individuals interact emotionally, which has become the media's goal. Instead of waiting for the natural expression of emotion, the digital giants look for ways to manufacture dissent. Any deviation from truth that works to protect this model is permissible. The truth in these media is only this information, which creates a strong emotional reaction. It is not surprising that anger, anxiety, and fear are emotions that guarantee a response from the audience. Fake news, propaganda, and lies attract more than facts and truth. Every new media repeats the propaganda model and protects the ideas of the community it represents, regardless of the truth and the facts of reality. These are the 'necessary illusions' that Chomsky spoke about in his 1989 book 'The Necessary Illusions: Control of Thought in Democratic Societies.'[8] Without creating and maintaining such illusions, it is impossible to maintain unity and consent in a human community. Is it possible for a democracy to exist without manipulating public opinion? Only if the media is democratised and civilian control over the mass media. According to Chomsky, in many cases, similar attempts in the United States are considered a violation of media freedom or a blow to their independence. The regulation of media activity is advertised as an attempt to restrict freedom of speech. Since there are no clear principles for choosing news topics, the mass media become a system without control. The media are dependent only on their owners, who are not responsible for the long-term effects of the content. Influencers and opinion leaders can manufacture dissent between the various groups to strengthen their power.

The democratic paradox is that without propaganda, present-day democracy starts to crumble. Once manufacturing consent is no longer possible, fragmentation occurs in the great society. Social media leads to a crisis of democracy. In the absence of organised propaganda that ideologically guides the masses in a liberal system, citizens are left to create their ideology. Necessary illusions work only inside the members of different hostile groups when freedom of opinion becomes freedom of belief. The division of smaller and smaller groups of people with a closer worldview is inevitable. Masses of people fall into a state of social inertia. In many cases, the possibility of identification through communication with other people is lost. The inertia is guided toward conflict as a new identification and social organisation. The system creates dissent between believers of hostile ideologies. The threat of an external enemy is instilled through vibrant and straightforward images that keep the virtual masses in combat readiness. The main problem of democracy has always been the doubt of people's ability to make sensible decisions on their own. Then the need for a leading educated elite emerges, without which chaos would ensue. Democracy becomes an oligarchy.

To govern with dissent

A normal democratic society must be based on consent, which is at the heart of social construction. So, consent and dissent of the masses are the main product of the media market in democracy. In his 1999 article 'Profit Over People: Neoliberalism and Global Order,'[9] Chomsky sees profit as the basic principle of the media. The pursuit of profit is often at the expense of conflict and dissent. The principle of 'consent of the governed' as a source of the legitimacy of the government is enshrined in the US Declaration of Independence. For this principle to work, the governed must have the right to consent and dissent. Dissent in a great society must be born of a desire for creativity and solidarity for the future of society. Dissent about the way how to achieve common goals and social prosperity. When this dissent is 'manufactured' and imposed for selfish purposes, it is destructive to the great society in the state. The problem with democracy is the extent to which it can allow dissent against the state's foundations without weakening unity and consent. In a democracy, people can be spectators with consent but not participants in the political and economic arena. In practice, this is a formal or staged democracy, and consent is only a voluntary waiver of rights.

Noam Chomsky believes that democracy can return to its basic idea of overcoming dissent through free dialogue between equal people. Democracy must be seen as a constant pursuit of an open discussion. Individuals are looking for ways to improve the social mechanisms that regulate their lives. Every social institution must deserve legitimacy through the consent of the governed. Since consent is still the primary source of legitimate power, manufacturing consent should be a primary task in each country. But what is the consent of the governed? The consent with whom? With the government or between all the governed? Is consent just an absence of political action? What if there is dissent but only with one political party or ideology? The best way for the government to survive dissent is to point it against a common enemy. If the ruling elite is split into parties, the energy of dissent can be diffused. This way, the status quo is protected, and the needed consent is manufactured on both sides. Propaganda gives the political parties and corporate interests a mechanism to throw masses against each other thus, the divide-and-rule model is at the heart of the democratic process. We can call it the manufacture of dissent. In the end, the result is consent because what is manufactured is passive spectators. The media's primary goal is to avert the attention of the masses in decision-making, especially in economic policies. Organisations responsible for the manufacture of dissent have financial interests and do not need to face the test of legitimacy. They can only profit from conflict, dissent, fear, and hate inside the public sphere. Cognitive infiltrations and covert operations are constantly in action in this Propaganda 2.0 media model. The Internet is the realm of moral anger that amplifies and spreads like a virus. The governed are left with no choice except to express their dissent. This expression creates counter-reaction and even more dissent. In this vicious cycle, if the government collapses, the next government faces the same amount of dissent. What follows is a new form of angry political passivity. The Propaganda 2.0 model favors private interests and looks like a winning model for everybody at the expense of social capital and national unity.

2.5. 'The end of history'—Francis Fukuyama

The end of history is a term introduced by Hegel and promoted by Alexandre Kojève, but gained popularity from the eponymous 1992 book 'The End of History and the Last Man'[10] by Francis Fukuyama. According to Fukuyama, history as a process with a specific goal has ended with the global adoption of the principles and ideals of liberal democracy. The 'end of history' primarily means the end of ideological battles. Liberal democracy has no ideological alternative, but that does not mean that it can be perceived as a global model. Instead, after its end, history can turn back to revive models from the past. Non-liberal democracy and banal nationalism, for example, are in some cases significantly better at producing consent. In response, the model of mass communication in liberal democracies stopped seeking consent and turned to dissent. It is a path away from democracy.

Fear and consent

For the Western ideology of neoliberalism, one of the great symbols of evil and an inexhaustible threat to freedom and democracy in the 20th century is communism. During the Cold War, communism played a key role as an antipode and balancer of the world's political and economic system. Without such a strong negative image of the universal enemy, liberal democracy seems incapable of reproducing its image as positive. Public opinion on key issues is most easily formed when there is some external threat. Otherwise, it disintegrates with the opinions of different groups and individuals. In 1970, Henry Kissinger declared that the threat of communism is constant: 'Today for the first time in our history, we face the stark reality that the communist challenge is unending.'[11] The mobilisation of public opinion in the name of consent deliberately maintains a sense of constant threat. The inertia of the old propaganda methods is still used in the new communication technologies. Demonising the image of the enemy still affects the masses. In the 21st century, the threat still comes from the communist challenge, although most communist and post-communist countries are already active participants in the global economy. Fukuyama notices a fact of the structure of totalitarian regimes of the 20th century, which other researchers often overlook. As in democracies, the principle of 'consent of the governed' also applies. It turns out that the 'manufacture of consent' is necessary for all countries, regardless of the form of government. Consent cannot be achieved by violence and coercion alone. It must be produced by the soft power of propaganda. Persuasion through mass media is working much better than old-school religious propaganda. The difference between dictatorship and democracy is mainly in how consent is produced. Coercion, censorship, and propaganda are used in the dictatorship. In a democracy, consent is manufactured by manipulating public opinion and democratic propaganda. In a dictatorship, citizens know that the media is in the service of power. In a democracy, it is important to maintain faith in independent media. Democratic media create a free space for discussions and expressions of individual opinions. In this space, public opinion should be naturally and independently formed. This belief is at the heart of democratic ideology. Even it works based on the suspension of disbelief and not in reality. The principle of consent in statehood rises above each ideology. Regardless of how the consent was manufactured, it must be accepted that the totalitarian states of communism governed with a certain dose of consent. Each country is a political community with an agreement between people on the political system's legitimacy. The regime's legitimacy does not stem from violence and coercion but from the social contract that the elites have concluded with the people. Fukuyama acknowledges the similarities in propaganda models for forming public opinion on both sides of the Iron Curtain. To be effective, propaganda always needs counter-propaganda. Every hero needs an antihero or a symbol of evil. However, the methods and technologies of propaganda are always the same. They seem to be above all morals and are ideologically neutral. The Cold War in the 20th century exhausted the possibilities of ideologies on both sides to create a positive image for the future. Citizens on both sides of the Iron Curtain are aware that their national propaganda has manipulated them. Mass media was the

58 Dissent and the theory of mass communication

language of power in the name of internal consent. After the end of the Cold War, this manipulation began to lose its effect. Civil Cold War online means that internal dissent erupts in both camps. One reason is that the Internet allows for quick access to information and verification of facts, making propaganda increasingly difficult to achieve on a large scale. Processes of partial democratisation in the media of the former authoritarian states follow. However, there are difficulties controlling and regulating Internet media in democracies. Eventually, the manufacture of dissent began on both sides of the Iron Curtain. Managing the masses' beliefs, convictions, thoughts, and opinions in countries is more difficult online. Despite the vast resources and all the new technologies, it can be said that attempts at total control of the human mind have failed so far. However, new forms of manipulation and propaganda emerge that target the audience as groups of individuals. The only chance is for the masses to be divided into hostile groups and thus controlled by constant conflict. Moral anger is provoked on the Internet and leads to fear and anxiety. The social groups online are a new virtual community made up of individualists. At the beginning of the 21st century, a new type of egoism emerged in social networks. One must rely mainly on oneself and build one's ideology of life. The ultimate individuality becomes a basic characteristic and goal of human existence in the new post-industrial information society. A new opportunity for manipulation and global influence through the Internet is born. Every country with political autonomy accepts new technologies for propaganda with fear. Despite globalisation's changes, the military threat remains a major stimulus for development, and the natural sciences produce historical change through military competition. Only the threat of war can force states to social reforms. In the age of global communications, information war and propaganda are becoming increasingly important. Countries that are not socially creative and do not have a single communication system are vulnerable to external propaganda attacks. Manufacturing consent creation is still a priority of the state and is carried out to protect foreign propaganda. The goal of conflict propaganda is always internal dissent and the division of society into groups. The paradox of war is that it guarantees the cohesion of society, even at the risk of its destruction. The threat of war is the greatest unifier of nations and the engine of technological and social progress. Fukuyama cites Kant and Hegel's observations of historical change, and that not the cooperation, but the conflict is the reason a person lives in societies: 'History proceeds through a continual process of conflict, wherein systems of thought as well as political systems collide and fall apart from their internal contradictions. They are then replaced by less contradictory and therefore higher ones, which give rise to new and different contradictions—the so-called dialectic.'[12] Dissent and conflict can also positively impact social creativity but only for a community of free individuals united by agreement on basic principles. Any human organisation that cannot create consent between its members according to basic principles is doomed to division and disintegration.

Conflicts in democracy

Liberal democracies won the Cold War in the 20th century to unite people of different backgrounds and interests. These countries are 'manufacturing consent' based on human freedoms and material prosperity. They formed a unified public opinion on all crucial issues through the mass media. But liberal democracy has the power to resolve social conflicts only if there is already a social morality and consensus on common values. According to Fukuyama, certain noneconomic problems such as inherited social status and nationality are unacceptable for democracy in many cases. The problem of democracy with traditional communities in different peoples is a problem with the formation of public opinion and 'manufacturing consent.' Propaganda and manipulation cannot change the opinion of conventional groups with a common history and a high degree of trust and cohesion within the group. In a liberal democratic society, individuals have opinions and make decisions according to their interests. Unlike more traditional societies, they do not defend the nation's interests or speak on its behalf. The development of liberal democracies is somewhat in conflict with the interests of nation-states. Governments are often forced to return to an illiberal strategy to maintain national unity. For Fukuyama, Democracy also cannot deal with disputes between different ethnic and national groups. An example is the issue of national sovereignty; it either belongs to one nation or another. Also, fundamental human rights cannot be universal if there is no universal state or power structure to protect them. Human rights also imply some obligations. In the social contract, the rights are received at the expense of the commitments. The mere conclusion of this treaty, whether with the tacit consent of the governed or with elections, is not sufficient for the state's existence. If the state exists only to respect human rights, it can seek another form of union in which those rights are protected. At the heart of the nation-state, there is always some ideal, a higher goal, and a cause. Their achievement unites the people in it. Without higher ideals and positive plans, the state is indifferent and loses its function. It has been replaced by international alliances and groups of individuals in which the relationship is purely economic. In a world that follows free-market principles, the pursuit of wealth as a higher goal for man is becoming an increasingly popular ideology. Consumerism is justified by self-interest as a rational choice.

The power of the powerless

The 15th chapter of 'The End of History' is called 'Vacation in Bulgaria,' and it quotes excerpts from the book by Vaclav Havel, 'The Power of the Powerless'[13] from 1980. In it, Havel gives a small illustration of what ideology is and how the manufacture of consent worked in communist Czechoslovakia. An example is a greengrocer, who surprisingly puts a slogan on the wall: 'Workers of the world, unite!' Of course, behind this benevolent act of obedience lies the truth, which is: I am afraid of power, and therefore I am submissive! If the greengrocer tells the truth, it will mean public shame and humiliation of his dignity. To save his public image, he must conditionally accept some high ideal. Even if this ideal is fake, it helps him shame his obedience. He hides behind something high. And this thing is called an ideology. Ideology is the high ideal behind which low passions and instincts must conceal. People's interests are the same, regardless of the political regime. Ideology is a slogan that everyone pretends to believe in, but not because it is so convincing. They demonstrate their faith publicly because it gives them social status. What's wrong with that? Asks the greengrocer his customers, who wonder why there is a political slogan over vegetables. The question perfectly illustrates the need for a high ideal in society. Something, at first glance, selfless and sound, in which we can pretend to believe. Wealth and high standards can never replace such ideals. The pursuit of comfort, luxury, and fame, for example, are individual ideals and have no public value. A group of people who dream of becoming rich and famous have nothing besides this common desire. They cannot live in a community based on such values. Trying to turn consumerism into an ideology leads to weakening relationships in societies. According to Havel, late socialism seeks to manufacture consent with the capitalist methods of consumerism. The totalitarian states of Brezhnev's time promised their citizens the fruits of western consumer culture like refrigerators or vacations in Bulgaria. The promise of material goods is used to buy public consent. The deal does not include a true national ideal and remains purely formal. Any breach of contract and material inconvenience leads to discontent against the state. For Havel, this is a Faust deal that turned the system's victims into its perpetrators. The state abdicates from the symbolic position of uniting and defending people in the name of national ideals, becoming simply a supplier of material goods. That is the beginning of the 'manufacturing consent' model in late socialism. The state begins to trade with consent. Logically, the business is superior to the state in this purely economic sphere. That is why some commercial corporations are becoming stronger and more efficient than entire countries. Private international companies achieved victory in the Cold War instead of Western states. The ability to form public opinion has led to the triumph of liberal democracy and the fall of the Iron Curtain. This victory was anti-ideological. It is a waiver of the slogan hanging in the greengrocer's shop in the name of the abundance of goods in it. According to Havel, many Eastern Europeans wanted the end of communism, not because of any high ideals but because of the living standards in West Germany. To this day, the standard of living in Germany and other Western countries is attracting millions of people from developing countries. People who are not as interested in political order and individual freedoms as in their material status. The choice of where to live is purely economic and has nothing to do with politics, ideology, religion, language, culture, and traditions. The ideology masks are down, and people choose identity because of amenities. What to be and where to live is already a commodity to buy. Citizens see no point in being in solidarity with the slogans of national ideology. People should be expected to do everything in the name of their rational interests, which, in some sense, means the end of the national consent system. The end of Fukuyama's history can also be seen as an end to ideology. The victory of liberal democracy turns out to be a Pyrrhic one. The 'rational devils' of the liberal state mark the manufacture of dissent based on extreme individualism. According to Fukuyama, the citizen of the liberal society is The Last Man of History: 'Lockean man did not need to be public-spirited, patriotic, or concerned for the welfare of those around him; rather, as Kant suggested, a liberal society could be made up of devils, provided they were rational.'[14]

2.6. 'Agenda setting'—Maxwell McCombs

Agenda-setting theory explores the media's power to prioritise society's agenda according to the agenda of its programs. Thus, they create news from specific topics and events by imposing them in the public space through their program. For viewers who see the world through the media, the agenda of the media program becomes a personal agenda for determining essential events in the world. The study of the manufacture of dissent is directly related to the media agenda. Consent and dissent can be suggested by systematic repetition of specific language constructions and images. According to this theory, mass media form the political reality, and the consent and unity in society depend on their messages. The approach of 'agenda-setting' was officially proposed by Maxwell McCombs and Donald Shaw in the 1968 Chapel Hill study[15] on media influence in attitudes toward the US presidential election. The study demonstrates a strong correlation between what a hundred people in Chapel Hill North Carolina think is most important in the election and what local and national media reports presented as the most important. The importance and significance of the problems in the news and their perception in society are compared. This way, McCombs and Shaw determine the extent to which the media form public opinion. The study 'The Agenda-Setting Function of Mass Media' was published in 1972, and despite much research on the subject after that, it remains relevant to date. The choice of news plays a huge role in shaping political reality. The audience is convinced of how important information is by its disposition toward others. In his 1922 book 'Public Opinion,' Walter Lippmann notices the power of the media over images in our heads and how they differ from the world outside. McCombs and Shaw develop this idea by observing that almost all political theater is only on the media stage. Outside of them, people have little information about political and social processes. The mass media becomes the only open space for contact between citizens and their representatives. Control over the program and the content of the media is control over the political reality in the heads of the audience.

62 Dissent and the theory of mass communication

McCombs and Shaw cite Bernard Cohen (The press and foreign policy, 1963), who, as early as 1963 claims, that the press is beginning to set the agenda for people's thoughts. You cannot tell people what to think, but what to think. The quality of the news chosen by the media is called 'Salience.' The primary influence of the media is in the role of road signs or posters, which announce the topics to be thought about and talked about. The agenda-setting theory hypothesizes that the mass media determine the degree of obviousness or Salience on issues. McCombs and Shaw's method simply compares preconceived notions and media messages. The focus covers the presidential election in Chapel Hill, California, between 18th September and 6th October, 1968. One hundred people were interviewed, and those who hesitated about whom to vote for were elected. Information was collected from all newspapers that published political and national newspapers, radio stations, and television. The conclusions are that voters tend to share a common opinion about what is essential with the media. This early study supports the hypothesis of 'agenda-setting' in the functions of the mass media. In addition to imposing topics and their importance, the media can block interest in other issues and events. Thus, setting the agenda at the second level also acts as 'framing,' restricting access and appealing to certain problems. The high level of the salience of the news is capable of stopping the need to acquire additional information on issues related to individual interests. That is a case of planned obsolescence of communication. A pseudo-communication that prevents you from being well-informed. In 1977 Maxwell McCombs published a solo article, 'Agenda-setting function of mass media.' The salience of a topic, the size of the title, and the frequent repetition suggest the issue's importance. Thus, the world in our heads is created from the media agenda, which we use. At the heart of the message is the very importance or salience. Like advertisements, they attract attention and suggest the importance of certain topics at the expense of others. The media act as a 'social radar' aimed not only at detecting and reporting but also at creating consensus on the importance of news. In this sense, 'agenda-setting' is linked to the model of manufactured consent. McCombs notes that opinion polls begin after 'important' topics have already been identified and imposed. The discussion limits are set without the right to choose and no possibility of discussing outside the headlines. In 1993, McCombs and Shaw issued an article 'The evolution of Agenda-Setting research: twenty-five years in the marketplace of ideas,' which describes the evolution of research on 'agenda-setting' over the years. They impose a new focus on these studies in connection with the increase in the role of the media and the interests behind them. The main focus is being removed from the public agenda because the media symbolises society. Today, it is more important who sets the media's agenda themselves and controls them. Thus, agenda-setting is linked to framing, and 'newsworthiness' is determined. This issue is key to the link between journalism and public relations. The question of newsworthiness is included in the motto of the New York Times: 'All the News That's Fit to Print.' So far, it is unclear what the criterion is for determining the 'fit' news. Thus, one of the oldest questions of journalism and the media about 'newsworthiness' remains open today. It could be assumed that the appropriate news is chosen at the will of the media owners. Their interests often dominate the interests of society and the state. The economic policy of online media is to keep people connected, and the best way to do it is by manufacturing dissent.

2.7. 'Pseudo news'—Niklas Luhmann

In 'The Spiral of Silence,' Elizabeth Noelle-Neumann quotes the 1971 book by German sociologist Niklas Luhmann called 'Politische Planung'[16] (Political planning). She notes the closeness between the ideas of Nicklas Luhmann and Walter Lippmann about the study of the manufacture of consent by simplifying the picture of the world and unifying opinions. Niklas Luhmann developed a concept of 'Public opinion' (Offentlichen meinung), where society's consent from reducing complexity to achieve communication and action. Luhmann and Lippmann agree that public opinion is manufactured as a way of public control. Niklas Luhmann is a representative of System Theory[17] in sociology, and for him, social systems are primarily systems of communication. Communication is between the system and the environment and between the subsystems and the groups inside the system. He introduces the term 'differentiation' in the sense of dividing the system into subsystems as a way to deal with the problem of increasing complexity. According to Luhmann, the division of the state into subsystems in the historical process creates a 'differentiated society.' In it, politics is separated from religion, and religion from science, science from education and art, and so on. When these subsystems become solid and complex enough, they exist independently. Then each subsystem starts to produce its reality, leading to the disintegration of the great system or the state and its unifying reality. The constant maintenance of living and active interconnections between the subsystems keeps the great social system alive and busy. Then the state follows the path to sociocultural evolution and social progress.

Self-monitoring management

In his book 'The Reality of the Mass Media'[18] (Die Realität der Massenmedien) from 1996, Nicklas Luhmann defines the function of mass media as 'self-monitoring management in the public system.' Mass media have the power to create a reality that individuals accept even though they know the mechanisms of its production. The truth and reliability of media messages play a minor role in choosing news and building a story. The task of the media is approaching narrative art and the creation of its meanings. These meanings serve as landmarks in the system of values. Before it is accurate and a moral assessment, news must be part of a connected and meaningful story. How does a topic become suitable for discussion by society? Formula words are used to make a topic worthy of discussion. The global media law is that the more massive the media audience becomes, the more limited the issues are and viewed more superficially. The system of society cannot deal with an indefinite number of different topics at once. In search of growing audiences, the media are losing their ability to create real publicity. For Luhmann, the function of public opinion is just to put a particular topic on the table for discussion. The public must pay attention because attention drives public opinion. The thematization of global mass media is becoming an automatic process in which the only task is to seek more attention and attract more viewers. The pursuit of publicity creates an imitation of publicity. Luhmann assumes that the political system is based on rules to attract attention. Rules must determine what to put for discussion and whatnot. Mass communication tools determine what to include in the agenda. They create and maintain the idea of publicity. The public itself is formed in this process of self-reflexivity through public expression on specific topics and monitoring this media image. In this process, the main goal is to attract attention, and the same interest and participation of individuals mean to create a community. Thus, manufacturing consent becomes a community production. After a discussion, interest in the topic began to decline, as did the community's cohesion. At this point, the mass media offer a new topic, and the process repeats itself. New ones cover old issues, and creating publicity is becoming increasingly difficult. This process is exacerbated by the advent of the Internet and the search for growing audiences, and the creation of virtual publicity.

The ideal complex social system

According to Luhmann, a large society can only exist as a system of rules. It is a system that allows all subsystems, groups, and individuals enough freedom to create and live in the realities they construct. The ideal complex social system enables the coexistence of many realities. Their existence in communication with each other creates a climate of social creativity. The ideal of cybernetics and virtual communities on the Internet is creating parallel realities in a system with common rules. The 'agenda-setting' and the 'pseudo-events' of the media in the form of news and crises create new 'pseudo realities.' The variety of orientation subsystems requires 'geographical maps' and 'road signs.' They simplify complexity and allow for easy choice of direction. This 'geographical map' defines the 'agenda-setting' of the mass media and the stereotypes, thematic, framing, and 'formula words.' For Niklas Luhmann, the choice of news, the point of view, and the topics discussed in the mass media form public opinion. The question of choosing topics and news in the mass media is a matter of the functions of the media in society.

Niklas Luhmann claims that 'the mass media's function consists of managing self-monitoring in the public system.'[19] Mass media should act as a mirror. The individual can see society as a complete system and its position. On the one hand, the mass media absorb communication and, on the other, stimulate it. The media connect the old and the new as the factor for social progress and produce meanings. According to Luhmann, a centuries-old tradition presents the media as unfavorable. The delusion that the stability of the social system depends only on consensus, the social contract, or the common faith of religion is suggested. Paradoxically all free media plays a destructive role in society as a system. Mass media can be a factor of destabilisation used only to destroy or replace these preconditions. Luhmann believes that the 'manufacture of consent' and the controlled maintenance of a moral consensus in society hinder social creativity and sustain progress. Dissent is the actual energy of change, and every system must channel that energy to maintain its development. Public consensus has been established in the past and does not address current problems and changes in the social system. According to Luhmann, in a complex and non-transparent system, communication is possible only in the presence of Dissent (Dissens). Even the dissent itself is a condition and a test of communication. For Luhmann, it is natural that the mass media construct new realities, especially in 'mass spread and anonymous perception.' He makes a paradoxical assumption about the impact and function of mass media in the 'production of nontransparency from transparency.' The media take clear facts and create vague opinions. The function of mass media is not in the production of publicity but in creating its vision. It doesn't represent reality but mainly the public's image as a whole. Luhmann calls this feature the manufacture of the future or creating a shared vision for the future. This public idea of society is its official image manufactured by the media. In it, all subsystems work, all groups are equal, and all individuals participate in the discussion. The media always present an ideal image of itself, and they rarely touch on topics related to their property and sponsorship. This way, the perfect image of publicity is preserved. The media mirrors society, but they also show themselves in it. This media image is highly manipulated. Society may have a negative side, but the media is always a positive force. According to Luhmann, this hypocrisy of the media cannot be avoided. The self-control of the media system is impossible due to the self-esteem of the media that they work in the service of society. The media themselves are deceived by the false image they build for themselves. The media mirror is always pink. This paradox is the basis of the planned obsolescence of mass media communication.

Second-degree cybernetics

Nicklas Lohmann asks a straightforward question about the reality of the mass media. If we get all the information about the world around us from the mass media, why can't we trust it completely? The mass media construct our reality, and we accept it, even though we are aware of manipulation mechanisms. This Luhmann paradox is called 'Second-order Cybernetics.'

He used the term introduced by Heinz von Forster in the 1974 'Cybernetics of Cybernetics' article. There is a difference between first-degree cybernetics (cybernetics of the observed system) and second-degree cybernetics (cybernetics of the monitoring system). Thus, the media, the science of communication, and sociology face a fictional image of society. They are exploring an image that they have constructed. How can information about the world and society be recognised as reality once it is known how it is produced? The paradox of 'second-degree cybernetics' noticed by Luhmann is surprisingly reminiscent of the phenomenon of 'kayfabe,' which is a form of 'hyper normalization' and euphemization of socially unacceptable facts. The problem of the manufacture of dissent is directly related to the questions posed by Niklas Luhmann. Once people know that they live in realities they have invented, why do they continue to produce dissent and conflict? He gave the example of the Gulf War and the criticism of mass media's biased and even scripted coverage. Perhaps this happened because the truth contradicted the media's understanding of what war should look like. When reality contradicts its media image, it causes cognitive dissonance. It seems natural for the media to start staging and directing the war to include it in their scenario for reality. Since war is the most horrible form of reality created by man, the possibility of directing it shows the unlimited power of the media. War is not accepted as a reality by the audience until the media cover it. Concludes Jean Baudrillard's famous essay 'The Gulf War did not take place' from 1995. Baudrillard claims that the Gulf War was not a real war but a media simulation. The essential thing in it is the construction of its media image. War is not so much against the enemy, but above all against the truth. It is a radical means of 'manufacturing consent.' In Niklas Luhmann's words, the truth aligns with the media's understanding.

2.8. 'Distorted communication'—Jürgen Habermas

In his 1991 book 'The structural transformation of the public sphere: An inquiry into a category of bourgeois society,' Jürgen Habermas sees the essence of the Enlightenment as a time for change. The human has already left his self-inflicted minor and is gradually entering a mature age. In man's maturity, he has to use his mind in public. Everyone is called to be a publicist who, through his writings, speaks to the world. This speaking to the world is happening in online media, where every publication is available worldwide. At the same time, a climate of dissent is being created due to the clash of millions of views. The transformation of the global communication network into an international open-access library is the most important event of the 21st century—a clear sign of humanity entering its mature age. Unfortunately, coming out of a minor is hampered by the planned obsolescence of communication. This communication puberty sabotages man's newly discovered independence and is the main reason for the manufacture of dissent.

Staging public opinion

Enlightenment is the way out of a person from a state in which someone else controls his mind. Self-inflicted minor is not a lack of reason, but determination and courage to use it without foreign leadership. Part of the democratic theory sees propaganda and the 'manufacture of consent' as the basis of the democratic process. Habermas commented on the outcome of this manipulation as a 'staged public opinion.' Staging is done through a simulated interest in a topic. Such staged public opinion is created to order and with a specific interest. It has a strong negative effect on local human communities. Staged opinion hinders spontaneous processes of communication, which are the basis for social creativity and progress. According to Habermas, publicity is returning to the age of communication feudalism. In this neo-feudalism, the leaders of public opinion and charismatic personalities rule many small groups in the torn kingdom of the great society. The consensus is created only based on common interests. For Habermas, the public relations industry and strategic communication have already acquired a political role. This new power imposes its communication model on the state itself. The way out of this feudality is for the state to act with business methods and treat individuals as consumers. The public relations sector has already adopted a political character. Businesses were the first to reflect the secret formula of power in the age of global communication on the Internet. Only in this way will the state, which claims public power legitimised by society, regain its publicity and new legitimacy for its power. In the information realm, customers are willing to follow the suppliers. The reclaim of publicity should be the primary goal of the state.

Habermas is critical of using staged public opinion to manipulate social control. Public opinion correlates domination and power, which exists only politically in the relationship between power and the people. Habermas uses the metaphor of public opinion as a possible force of friction that the government can control by applying the necessary lubricant. Thus, the government provides support and legitimacy from the public. As an instrument of power, the main task of public opinion is to bring harmony to all different opinions and disagreements. The consent is always manufactured from a position of strength. This position of power is at the heart of public opinion. Public opinion has the same power in political campaigns and product advertising. Once relationships in groups and society have broken down, individuals become susceptible to instilling opinions. Publicly manifested opinions replaced public opinion. An audience of disorganised private people replaced society. They are committed not to public communication, but to the communication of publicly obsessed opinions. This disturbing finding means trends for the gradual transformation of human society into a collection of individuals with common characteristics. It requires the creation of methods for measuring the degree of publicity of a member audience and its connection with external media publicity. 'Public' is opposed to 'mass' in the search for empirically applicable criteria for defining public opinion. Many fewer people express an opinion in the mass than those who perceive it. The public has become an abstract collection of individuals receiving mass media impressions. Predominant communications are organised to distort-free personal opinions. Mass opinion is created by control of the expression by the authorities.

Pseudo-communication of the virtual masses

The main difference between 'public' and 'mass' is in the ways of producing consensus and conflict. Public opinion expresses a moral consensus with the direct and free exchange of views. It is a consequence of an individual compromise of each person in the name of unity and consent. The process is similar in the mass of people but includes only elites and leaders of society. They create consensus among themselves and impose it on the majority. This 'manufacture of consent' means social peace and order but at the expense of the existence of the community itself. The price is the loss of connections and feelings created in interpersonal communication. This domination and power are subject to a change in the 'structural change of bourgeois public sphere' of which Habermas speaks. The model of domination and power leads to a 'Systematically distorted communication,' according to his 1970 article. In many cases, the failure to decipher messages in mass communication is the damaged speech that mass media and institutions use. In interpersonal communication, each word is directed to a direct interlocutor. In mass communication, words act as commands to a mass of people. The feedback is in the simple reaction or the execution of the commands. This damage to living human speech interferes with any kind of linguistic analysis, interpretation, or translation. In this case, the incomprehensibility results from a damaged organisation of the speech itself. The structure of the message is entirely subordinate to the principles of domination and power instead of communication. Habermas calls this 'pseudo communication,' an action that only resembles and is considered proper communication. Pseudo-communication does not lead to understanding, sharing, and reciprocity between the participants. It creates mutual disturbances and misunderstandings, which the participants take as a consensus. Only neutral observers notice that they do not understand each other. This illusion of the reality of pseudo-communication is so strong that Habermas compares it to the concept of 'pseudonormality.' Freud's concept derives from his observations of sleep. Habermas believes that it can be used in social psychology and the study of systematically distorted communication. Pseudonormality is expressed in a hidden pathology of collective behavior and entire social systems. Habermas compares the questions 'What?' and 'Why?' in the study of systematically distorted communication. It is not so important what is reported, but why? What is the effect that is sought, and who benefits from it? Distortion is not accidental and always has a specific purpose. It is not just a misunderstanding or confusion, but a deliberate action with negative results for the community. Pseudo-communication, after all, creates an illusion of community, a staged public from alienated individuals. This intentionally distorted communication is available for 'translation,' but only for the informed part of the elites, who understand the language of domination and power of the mass media. It is time for the language of power to be translated.

The language of power

Alan Gross developed Habermas' idea of 'distorted communication' in his 2010 article, 'Systematically distributed communication: An impediment to social and political change.' According to him, in distorting communication, one of the parties is in a state of self-deception. Therefore, recognition and criticism alone are not enough. Timely action must be taken against such a state. Alan Gross gave a few examples of such a dangerous distortion as the total imposition of the Nazi language in Europe during World War II and biased practices for prescribing by American doctors influenced by the promotions of pharmaceutical companies. The most dangerous manipulation for society is that communication participants act in a state of self-delusion. People believe that they can make their own decisions and choose their own opinions, but just carry out commands. The ideal of manipulation and propaganda is when people are reduced to machines. They can install different software that they will follow as an innate instinct. In the 'manufacturing consent' model, the authorities state that consent is 'staged.' Unlike dictatorship and totalitarian regimes in democracy, the masses delude that power is in their hands. This self-delusion is at the heart of the legitimacy of power in a democracy. Manipulation is associated with fraud but systematically distorted communication with self-delusion. Habermas' focus on personality and family gives him a reason to transfer his interest in society and look for typical models. In an interesting observation from 1971, Habermas compares institutions in society with neuroses:

'But if the basic conflict is defined by the conditions of material labor and economic scarcity, i.e., the shortage of goods, then the renunciations it imposes are a historically variable factor. The pressure of reality and the corresponding degree of societal repression then depend on the degree of technical control over natural forces and the organisation of their exploitation, and the distribution of the goods produced. The more the power of technical control is extended, and the pressure of reality decreases, the weaker becomes the prohibition of instincts compelled by the system of self-preservation: The organisation of the ego becomes correspondingly stronger, along with the capacity to master denial rationally. It suggests a comparison of the world-historical process of social organisation with the individual's socialisation process. As long as the pressure of reality is overpowering and ego organisation is weak, instinctual renunciation can only be brought about by the forces of affect, the species finds collective solutions for the problem of defense, which resemble neurotic solutions at the individual level. The same configurations that drive the individual to neurosis move society to establish institutions. What characterises institutions is at the same time what constitutes their similarity with pathological forms.'[20]

In Volume 2 of 'The Theory of Communicative Action,'[21] he developed the idea that the pathology of the institutions is in the firmness of their opinions and answers. The neurotic recurrence of actions is also symptomatic, which generates distorted communication. Regardless of reality, some neurotics feel compelled to repeat their steps constantly, so some economies or media create content for sale, whether consumers want or can afford it. As Nazi language and biased drug prescription practices, these pathologies are the subjects of Alan Gross's research. In politics and social practice, these distortions are analogous to mental neuroses. Such shared networks of conviction and self-delusion hinder change and have the purpose of justifying inequalities in power in economic, social, and political life. They seek to maintain the status quo they benefit from. Distorted communication excludes critical debate. It hinders free access to information and imposes isolation through a closed language. It prevents people from reaching a consensus on their own. Political regimes deliberately distorted communication and set a language of domination and power. Thus, they create a pseudo-normality to legitimise their actions. The most significant 'achievement' in this closed language is introducing a majority into self-delusion. The masses believe that they control communication, make decisions, choose topics, and form opinions. Ideology is an illusion that is ensured by the power of shared beliefs. Ideologies create systematically distorted communication which is the linguistic expression of power. This language of domination and power was deliberately created by changing the meanings and connections between existing words. The goal is to achieve the effect of self-delusion on those who use it. Language is a Trojan horse for penetrating ideology into this part of the psyche, which was previously a personal and intimate space. Language has the power to create a reality in which any action can be justified. With a fully consciously organised strategy, Nazi German propaganda minister Goebbels and party philosopher Rosenberg created 'The Language of the Third Reich'[22] as a conscious product of Nazi propaganda. Through this new language, most Germans themselves are brought into conditions for self-delusion. They did not understand that they were charged with Nazi ideology and thought they were telling the truth itself on their behalf. Even when they were aware that there were repressive intentions in the language of Nazism, the language itself instilled conviction that their victims were guilty and deserved their fate. There is no room for criticism in systematically distorted communication generated by a specially designed and systematically imposed language. All words in this language are commands and are beyond doubt. The ideal form of pseudonormality is when people 'are convinced that they were not convinced.' In addition to political ideologies, Alan Gross found this type of self-delusion in business practices, such as drug promotions among doctors. A study[23] from 1992 shows that after returning from paid conferences in luxury hotels, the doctors prescribed more drugs from the sponsor company. Still, they deny that they have changed their opinion. It is a case of suspension of normality. There's no such thing as a free lunch.

Pseudonormality

The conclusions of these studies show that within a language community, all actions inadmissible for external morality can be justified by language constructions. It allows for manipulation with a remarkable effect and controls the consciousness, through which the understandings of good and evil are regulated. The formation of public opinion and public morality governs the behavior and views of individuals in the community. Thus, the language of domination and power, with the help of controlled mass media, creates a 'pseudo society.' It is united around an ideology composed of a submissive mass of people who carry out commands, convinced that these are their desires and needs. The danger of this technology of mass persuasion is that professionalism and intelligence cannot protect individuals from self-delusion when their interests are satisfied. It is shown by research into immoral business practices related to drug promotions among doctors. Manipulation creates cohesion and consent of a group of people at the expense of unhappiness and harm to another group in society. All this is morally justified by self-delusion. Alan Gross concludes that 'systematically distorted communication' is primarily organised. It is done with the support of the institutions in the hierarchical structure of society. The study of this phenomenon is complicated by the impossibility of self-reflexing of the affected individuals and institutions. The change can only come with a new distribution of power to access information. Redistribution will mean a new information order and information equality. Alan Gross concludes that if power is not redistributed, such a social, political, and economic change cannot happen. In totalitarian regimes, this cannot happen without some form of violence. In democratic regimes, there is a chance that citizens will turn to power without violence and demand a fairer information order. Citizens can organise, lobby, protest, vote, and create their communication networks. In this direction, the Internet and the development of virtual communities have a huge impact. There, everyone has the right to participate in the discussion, which is free from the language of power. However, all archives of historical cases of self-delusion and fabrication of public morals are available on the Internet. The change must begin with a reassessment of the old ideologies. Creating a new language of equality and sharing must replace the language of domination and power of the past. The media language of power affects vast masses of people, imitating the language of the community and speaking on behalf of 'We.' It is the language of the power elites, which spreads among the vast majority and speaks on its behalf in a situation of 'pseudo communication.' The change in the communication model is, above all, a change in public speech and the strategy with which words in mass media become political and economic actions. The language of the mass media is always the bearer of public morality and contains a moral assessment of all the topics discussed. Various ideologies collide in moral systems in the climate of disagreement created by the systematic distortion of communication on the mass media stage. The significant change in the propaganda model is from 'manufacturing consent' to 'divide and rule online' as a form of social control. In the global world, the big winners of this model of dissent are digital corporations, for which anger and disagreement mean more profit. Human 'traffic' is what the media trades on the Internet. Advertisers buy time spent in the media space regardless of the reason for interest and the topic of the messages. Thanks to distorted communication, propaganda, manipulation, false news, and disinformation, the dissent model works. Empirical indicators for this model can easily be found using methods for linguistic analysis of the language of power in the mass media. It is the moral resilience of new generations of media researchers to challenge the power of the digital giants. Otherwise, democratic achievements in mass communication will be lost in the approaching digital neo-feudalism. It looks like in the virtual realm of the Fifth Estate, Fukuyama is not right about the end of history. There can be a regress from liberal democracy to an alternative system.

Notes

1 Lippmann, Walter. (1920). *Liberty and the news*. New York: Harcourt, Brace and Howe.
2 Lippmann, W. (1946). *Public opinion*. Brunswick, NJ: 1991 by Transaction Publishers (Originally published by the Macmillan Company in 1922).
3 Bernays, Edward. (1961). *Crystallizing public opinion*. New York: Liveright.
4 Bernays, Edward. (1928). *Propaganda*. New York: Liveright.
5 Bernays, E. L. (1928). Manipulating public opinion: The why and the how. *American Journal of Sociology*, 33(6), 958–971.
6 Noelle-Neumann, E. (1993). *The spiral of silence: Public opinion: Our social skin*. Chicago: University of Chicago Press.
7 Chomsky, N. (2002). *Media control: The spectacular achievements of propaganda* (Vol. 7). New York: Seven Stories Press.
8 Chomsky, N. (1995). *Necessary illusions: Thought control in democratic societies*. Toronto: House of Anansi.
9 Chomsky, Hoam. (1999). *Profit over people: Neoliberalism and global order*. New York: Seven Stories Press.
10 Fukuyama, F. (2006). *The end of history and the last man*. New York: Simon and Schuster.
11 Kissinger, Henry. (1977). The permanent challenge of peace: US policy toward the Soviet Union. *American Foreign Policy*, NY, p. 302.
12 Fukuyama, F. (2006). *The end of history and the last man*. New York: Simon and Schuster.
13 Havel, V., and P. Wilson. (1985). The power of the powerless. *International Journal of Politics*, 15(3/4), 23–96.
14 Fukuyama, F. (2006). *The end of history and the last man*. New York: Simon and Schuster.

15 McCombs, M. E., and D. L. Shaw. (1972). The agenda-setting function of mass media. *Public Opinion Quarterly*, 36(2), 176–187.
16 Luhmann, Niklas. (1971). *Politische Planung. Aufsätze zur Soziologie von Politik und Verwaltung*. Opladen: Westdeutscher Verlag.
17 Luhmann, N. (1982). The world society as a social system. *International Journal of General Systems*, 8(3), 131–138.
18 Luhmann, N. (1995). Die realität der massenmedien. In *Die Realität der Massenmedien*, pp. 5–73. Wiesbaden: VS Verlag für Sozialwissenschaften.
19 Luhmann, N. (1995). Die realität der massenmedien. In *Die Realität der Massenmedien*, pp. 5–73. Wiesbaden: VS Verlag für Sozialwissenschaften.
20 Habermas, Jürgen. (1971). *Knowledge and human interests*. Trans. Jeremy J. Shapiro. Boston: Beacon Press, p. 276.
21 Habermas, J. (1985). *The theory of communicative action: Volume 2: Lifeworld and system: A critique of functionalist reason* (Vol. 2). Boston: Beacon Press.
22 Klemper, Victor. (2002). *The language of the third reich*. London: Continuum.
23 Orlowski, J. P., and L. Wateska. (1992). The effects of pharmaceutical firm enticements on physician prescribing patterns: There's no such thing as a free lunch. *Chest*, 102(1), 270–273.

Reference list

2. Dissent and the theory of mass communication

2.1. 'Manufacturing consent'—Walter Lippmann

Lippmann, Walter (1920). *Liberty and the news*. New York: Harcourt, Brace, and Howe.
Lippmann, Walter (1946). *Public opinion*. Brunswick, NJ: 1991 by Transaction Publishers (Originally published by the Macmillan Company in 1922).

2.2. 'Democratic propaganda'—Edward Bernays

Bernays, E. L. (1928). Manipulating public opinion: The why and the how. *American Journal of Sociology*, 33(6), 958–971.
Bernays, E. L. (1947). The engineering of consent. *The Annals of the American Academy of Political and Social Science*, 250(1), 113–120.
Bernays, Edward (1928). *Propaganda*. New York: Liveright.
Bernays, Edward (1961). *Crystallizing public opinion*. New York: Liveright.

2.3. 'The spiral of silence'—Elizabeth Noelle-Neumann

Noelle-Neumann, E. (1993). *The spiral of silence: Public opinion—Our social skin*. Chicago: University of Chicago Press.

2.4. 'Propaganda model'—Noam Chomsky and Edward Herman

Chomsky, Hoam (1999). *Profit over people: Neoliberalism and global order*. New York: Seven Stories Press.
Chomsky, N. (2002). *Media control: The spectacular achievements of propaganda* (Vol. 7). New York: Seven Stories Press.

Chomsky, N. (1995). *Necessary illusions: Thought control in democratic societies.* Toronto: House of Anansi.

Chomsky, N., & E. S. Herman (1994). *Manufacturing consent: The political economy of the mass media.* London: Vintage Books.

2.5. 'The end of history'—Francis Fukuyama

Fukuyama, F. (2006). *The end of history and the last man.* New York: Simon and Schuster.

Havel, V., & P. Wilson (1985). The power of the powerless. *International Journal of Politics,* 15(3/4), 23–96.

Kissinger, Henry (1977). The permanent challenge of peace: US policy toward the Soviet Union. *American Foreign Policy,* NY, p. 302.

2.6. 'Agenda setting'—Maxwell McCombs

McCombs, M. (1977). Agenda setting function of mass media. *Public Relations Review,* 3(4), 89–95.

McCombs, M. E., & D. L. Shaw (1972). The agenda-setting function of mass media. *Public Opinion Quarterly,* 36(2), 176–187.

McCombs, M. E., & D. L. Shaw (1993). The evolution of agenda-setting research: Twenty-five years in the marketplace of ideas. *Journal of Communication,* 43(2), 58–67.

2.7. 'Pseudo news'—Niklas Luhmann

Luhmann, Niklas (1971). *Politische Planung. Aufsätze zur Soziologie von Politik und Verwaltung.* Opladen: Westdeutscher Verlag.

Luhmann, Niklas (1982). The world society as a social system. *International Journal of General Systems,* 8(3), 131–138.

Luhmann, Niklas (1995). Die realität der massenmedien. In *Die Realität der Massenmedien,* pp. 5–73. Wiesbaden: VS Verlag für Sozialwissenschaften.

2.8. 'Distorted communication'—Jürgen Habermas

Boyd-Barrett, O. (2016). *Western mainstream media and the Ukraine crisis: A study in conflict propaganda.* Abingdon, UK: Routledge.

Gross, A. G. (2010). Systematically distorted communication: An impediment to social and political change. *Informal Logic,* 30(4), 335–360.

Habermas, J. (1970). On systematically distorted communication. *Inquiry,* 13(1–4), 205–218.

Habermas, J. (1971). *Knowledge and human interests.* Trans. Jeremy J. Shapiro. Boston: Beacon Press, p. 276.

Habermas, J. (1985). *The theory of communicative action: Volume 2: Lifeworld and system: A critique of functionalist reason* (Vol. 2). Boston: Beacon Press.

Habermas, J. (1991). *The structural transformation of the public sphere: An inquiry into a category of bourgeois society.* Cambridge, MA: MIT Press.

Klemper, Victor (2002). *The language of the third reich.* London: Continuum.

3 Digital media as a risk to democracy

Peter Ayolov

3.1. Digital capitalism and decorative democracy

Digital capitalism

In 2016, Oliver Boyd-Barrett's study 'Western mainstream media and the Ukraine crisis: A Study in Conflict Propaganda,'[1] there is an interesting observation about the industrial spirit for the manufacture of information and the emergence of a new kind of capitalism. The mass media needs constant dissent and conflict to create unique content. This principle is above all ideology and national interest. Dissent and conflict are designed to control the continuous flow of information. Media content just serves this continuous flow. As a language of power, the media is providing a communication infrastructure. The content of the media as an integral part of the economic system of mass communication leads to the idea of a new 'digital capitalism.' Those who can ensure the spread of their ideas in society also control the media. In the case of the media coverage of the 2014 crisis in Ukraine, publications on the Internet are not looking for a solution to conflict and clarity of information. Instead, they exacerbate the confusion and fuel the conflict between the two camps for higher internet traffic. From the point of view of the online media business, the constant production of conflict is the best strategy. It is much more of a marketing technique than a political position of the editorial office. Media owners require more profits, which requires more publications on each topic. By dramatising events and inciting conflict, audiences focus on an issue for the longest possible period. Digital capitalism is a definition introduced by Dan Schiller in his eponymous 1999 book 'Digital capitalism: Networking the global market system.' According to Schiller, 'digital capitalism' instead of regulating and balancing the market system is increasingly exacerbating the inequality and dominance of the elite. The digital economy is gradually taking over education, the media, and even science. Thus, it imposes the market model everywhere in its digital form. The development of the Internet is a perfect example of neoliberal ideology. The Internet relies on a lack of regulation and the creation of conditions for the constant growth of the economy

DOI: 10.4324/9781003380207-4

in the endless network of information. Corporations themselves and businesses, in general, are beginning to follow the principles of this developing network society. Gradually, the Internet became the central space of business communications, which is the beginning of digital capitalism. This new capitalism is supranational, and its goal is to constantly increase the amount of information transferred to its controlled communication network. Digital capitalism is the dream market utopia because it offers endless growth in cyberspace. The Internet traffic principle works quantitatively and considers the amount of information transmitted between users, regardless of content. Information merchants buy and sell this traffic, ensuring that their ads and PR messages reach the maximum number of users. The market principle of Internet media in 'digital capitalism' is self-sufficient. Truth and the pursuit of balance and consent have no role in it. Not if they do not create traffic. The dramatisation of events, conflict propaganda, and false news have a much better effect on attracting audiences' interest. These communication distortions are used more as marketing approaches than as part of any policy strategy. Online pseudo-communication turns out to be very profitable. In his 2015 article called 'Digital capitalism: stagnation and contention,'[2] Dan Schiller warns of how digital capitalism is tearing apart the structure of democracy. Polarising public opinion and publishing radical opinions is the easiest way to gain audiences' attention. If it wants to keep its audiences, the media must fiercely defend the positions and ideologies they have been attracted to. It is often at the expense of open conflict with other media outlets. Dissent from other people's opinions becomes a way to identify and consolidate one's position. The constant war of opinion between hostile groups in the media is gradually becoming an identification model.

The new media model for manufacturing dissent weakens social capital and trust in nation-states and benefits individual and corporate interests. On the Internet, people increasingly doubt official information. Easy access to all the world's digital archives creates a world without secrets, and along with the freedom to invent endless conspiracy theories, it seriously shakes the status quo. Every centralised government is based on secrets and restrictions of public information. What and to what extent can people be told is the first and foremost question in the traditional information system. The goal is to preserve public morality, consent, and unity, which is no longer possible in a culture where all facts seem to be available. To a large extent, this age of revelation means the end of political illusions and ideologies. There is a severe crisis of the legitimacy of democracy due to the lack of the consent of the governed. The danger of these processes is from the return of anti-democratic models of government in a democratic way. Formal democracies are being created that cover up authoritarian regimes and oligarchies. It can be argued that the market model of online media leads to strong anti-democratic trends, and this is a risk to democracy.

Decorative democracy

Awareness of this crisis of liberal democracy in the context of the Internet leads to a need to change the old paradigm of communication. The process of change is two-sided and has effects beyond the democratic community. The Internet makes it possible to impose a model of a 'pseudo communication' in which the consent of the governed is produced by manipulation. On the one hand, this model includes authoritarian trends and unofficial control of information in democracies. On the other hand, there is an apparent liberalisation of communication in traditional authoritarian regimes and the search for democratic development. 'Surveillance capitalism' means comprehensive monitoring of personal information and censorship of politically incorrect information. There is talk of a 'decorative' or 'managed' democracy in authoritarian countries. The liberalisation and privatisation of information control systems on the Internet is a double-edged sword. On the one hand, it gives everyone equal access to information and communication. On the other hand, it enables corporations to control and monitor individuals. As if, to avoid criticism and accusations of authoritarianism, the democratic state has abdicated and 'outsourced' the monitoring of the citizens of digital corporations. According to Evgeni Morozov, the great danger of digital capitalism is the growth of digital communication corporations, hence the title of his 2017 article, 'Moral panic over fake news eats the real enemy—the digital giants.' Democracy is plunged into fake news, and instead of looking for guilt in foreign propaganda, attention must be paid to the profits from the production of fake but 'click-worthy stories.' According to Morozov, the great threat to the West today is not the emergence of illiberal democracy abroad but the consolidation of immature democracy at home. This immaturity is illustrated by the misunderstanding of the elites that every social problem has an economic origin. The problem is also the distrust of the elite in professional expertise and media research. The problem is not in the false news itself but in the quantity and speed of its distribution. This cover with false information is extremely profitable for digital giants like Facebook and Google. For Morozov, the solution to the problem of fake news must be a market one, not political. It includes control and regulation of online ads, thus limiting the demand for traffic through sensational news. In confirmation of Morozov's concern, the US media corporations have made record profits since the fierce election battle between Hillary Clinton and Donald Trump.[3] Clinton and Trump's presidential campaigns are a clear example of the manufacture of dissent model. It follows a long tradition that leads to strong division in the American nation. According to a study by the Public Religion Research Institute (PRRI), called 'The Divide Over America's Future: 1950 or 2050?',[4] Americans are divided into two groups with opposite values and visions for the country's future. Digital corporations, such as Facebook, are directly accused of profiting from fake news and manufacturing dissent. They are forced to regulate the content of publications, impose censorship, and control online advertising. In 2017 Twitter co-founder Evan Williams[5] admitted to CNN that digital giants make money from fake news, and their creators are in many cases also motivated primarily by profit. CNN's documentary 'The fake news machine: Inside a town gearing up for 2020,'[6] tells the story of Mirko Ceselkoski from the town of Veles in Macedonia. He creates sites with fake political news for the American public and is already preparing for the next elections. The irony in this film is that CNN won a record $1 billion during the election, while Macedonian fake news authors earned a thousand dollars a month.

Such cases alert us to the danger of unregulated information on the Internet. In the existing economic system, information and an instrument of state power are also subject to trade. To increase the price, access to verified facts is limited. Information control is at the heart of any power. Any awkward truth and politically incorrect reality must be filtered. Otherwise, national history itself and the ideals that support the nation are threatened by this paradox of democracy. How to observe the principles of freedom of speech and at the same time manufacture the consent of the governed? The possibility of free information illuminated state power mechanisms, which inevitably led to losing her strength and legitimacy. Return to a censorship system is impossible. Propaganda and manipulation are becoming less effective. The traditional political models of the 20th century face the need for change. They can no longer produce the consent of the rulers and legitimise their power. Unfortunately, this change is not about seeking a fairer information order of equality and free sharing. Instead, power communication systems change their characteristics in an attempt to maintain the status quo. On the one hand, in liberal democracies such as the United States, the crisis of fake news, hybrid information war, and conflict propaganda has led to the need for more regulation and censorship of independent media. On the other hand, the spread of the Internet in 'formal democracies' such as China has led to comparative liberalisation in the field of public communication. In other countries, such as Indonesia and Russia, the 'managed democracy' model is applied, which seems to occupy the ideas of Walter Lippmann and Edward Bernays. Thus, one of the early ideas of democratic theory is revived and worked effectively in certain countries. The concept of the need for 'democratic propaganda' and 'manufacture of consent' tests the communication theory in liberal democracies and reveals global mass media's 'propaganda model.' The lack of regulations in Internet media allows for the use of the propaganda model for both economic and political gains. Corporate and business interests find an extremely favorable environment for high ratings and internet traffic. In most cases, they are not interested in the consequences for human communities. Through conflict propaganda and the guise of ideology, economic interests can incite large groups of people to dissent, hatred, violence, and even war. The problem with the manufacture of dissent is not a problem of the mass media but the development of democracy. Democratic countries need free media to have a healthy civil society.

In the media, individuals freely form and express their opinion. At the same time, the freer the control of the state is the media, the more they strive for profit at all costs. Imperceptibly, they become an arena of a war of opinion that produces disagreement between different communities. Thus, the government is entirely subject to changeable public opinion. They can hardly pursue a long-term policy without taking into account its dynamics. In an extreme phase of dissent, the existence of a united society and the legitimacy of power in the nation-state is called into question. That is the paradox of democracy, which strengthens the pattern of dominance in communication in the face of chaos. The actual democratic change would mean information equality and decentralisation of the global communication system. So far, there are no indicators of such trends.

3.2. Trust and dissent in democracy

Social capital

The Internet is putting democracy before the old problem of inequality described since Aristotle's time. In his 2013 book 'Power systems: Conversations on global democratic uprisings and the new challenges to the US empire,'[7] Noam Chomsky spoke about the common problem of democracy faced by Aristotle the 'father of logic' and James Madison the 'father of the American constitution.' The two offer completely different methods for solving it. In his 'Politics,' Aristotle argues that democracy is better than the oligarchy, but there is one big problem: inequality in material conditions and property. If nonproprietary free citizens vote in their interest, they could take away the property of the richest of them. For Aristotle, the solution to this problem is to reduce inequality in society. James Madison faces the same problem in the United States. According to him, however, democracy should be limited instead of inequality. Madison imposes the so-called Madisonian model, in which power is in the hands of the Senate, whose members are wealthy landowners and defend their interests. Today, the same problem is returning through virtual space and intellectual property protection technologies on the Internet. The Madisonian model is applied to wealthy media owners who defend their interests. Digital capitalism confronts democratic theory with social and information and digital inequality, leading to a loss of social capital. Distrust in society is one of the adverse effects of increased inequality in every area. In mass communication, trust results from spontaneous communication, which 'manufacturing' strategies exclude. There is trust between individuals if consent and dissent are natural and intuitive. It is possible in a society with a direct and open connection. What unites individuals in a democratic society is not just their shared ideas, beliefs, and opinions. On the contrary, it is the ability to live together despite disagreement and agree on essential issues for community life. Trust in each other is, above all, a desire for community and is beyond opinion and consent.

The problem is exacerbated because internet technology gives easy access to statistics on inequality. In the age of the Internet, social and information disparities cannot be hidden. Privileged elites are forced to use propaganda, PR, and advertising strategies to justify their situation. Thus, the natural and spontaneous connection is disrupted by the distorted communication of the mass media. Once information censorship is impossible on the Internet, all covert operations become public information one day. That makes it impossible to maintain the trust of the masses in the integrity of the government elites. The same goes for media owners, businesses, and the financial world. Ruling elites can no longer rely on the propaganda model and 'manufacturing consent' in the Internet media. The model must be turned into deliberate manufacture of dissent using the divide-and-rule model to maintain the status quo. The propaganda strategies for 'manufacturing' consent are changed to dissent. A real civil war on certain ideological boundaries begins in the media. However, this has just a temporary effect and creates tension. The distrust is contained in the meaning of the word 'manufacture.' In the original term 'Manufacture of consent' by Walter Lippmann, the meaning of the word 'manufacture' is in the sense of 'something done by hand.' However, in Edward Bernays' 'Engineering consent,' 'to engineer' means 'to arrange, to lead or manage' (arrange, guide or manage, contrast, construct), and 'to seduce, to deceive, to deceive '(seduce, trick, deceive). It is a massive contradiction in the democratic theory of public opinion, which openly accepts the 'manufacturing' of consent as a mass delusion and manipulation method. The produced pseudo-connection between individuals eventually gives birth to mistrust and destroys relationships in society. Both models of manipulation or 'manufacturing' of public opinion are delusion and fraud and pose a risk to both the cohesion of society and democracy. They must be assessed according to the degree of social trust they create. Francis Fukuyama addressed the problem of trust between individuals in a community in his 1995 book of the same name, 'Trust: Human nature and the reconstitution of social order.' Trust between people in a community is the ultimate goal of a traditional communication system. It creates connections between individuals and groups in society and gives rise to spontaneous communication without a centralised system of domination and power. Its main goal is a common understanding and social peace. This traditional communication goes beyond politics, trade, religion, and ideology and cannot be imitated or imposed externally. At its core are spontaneity and direct interpersonal relationships. The government and the power institutions cannot rule out the emergence of trust between the people by law. A traditional communication system covers the entire way of life of individuals. A thriving civil society depends on people's habits and customs. Their position in society, family, profession, and the groups they are members of is essential. These spontaneous relationships and relationships provide a solid foundation in the individual's life and create a sense of trust between him and other people. In the great society of nation-states, this spontaneity of relations is disturbed and leads to what Emil Durkheim calls 'Anomie.' It is a state in which society provides little moral guidance to individuals, no solid public opinion, and public morality. No mechanism guarantees the relationship between individuals and groups and creates a sense of security and trust in society. Trust as a social category is the primary goal of any social activity. It also applies to the economy because it is the basis for its well-being and ability to compete with other nations.

Unwritten rules and taboos based on public morality operate in the traditional system. Despite their repressive role, they are a reason for the desire of individuals to live in a community. The pursuit of community is a pursuit of rules and norms, not freedom and individuality. Society needs some common and great ideas to follow. Without the norms of society, one is left without a moral compass and feels lost. The propensity to create communities is related to Fukuyama's 'social capital.' This capital is something valuable that has been collected for generations. Social capital serves as insurance in times of moral crisis. Maintaining its high level is the result of spontaneous communication. However, the lack of a collective desire to create a community lacks social capital. Virtual spaces allow for the creation of new communities and groups in the great society of the state. If this is a spontaneous process, it would mean a high degree of trust and social capital. The Internet gives freedom for social experiments and returns to primary forms of public construction. A high degree of spontaneous communication and trust in the small groups is observed. They media the great society maintain a system of direct connections. Maintaining the independence and cohesion of small groups in a large community is at the heart of social construction. The mass society is built on a system of small and cohesive groups whose members are interconnected through generations with respect and moral values. This spontaneous communication and relationship of trust help economic development and social progress. Small communities are connected in some natural networks through which deals can be made, friendships can be made, and ideas exchanged between individuals. Interestingly, despite voluntary membership, individuals strictly adhere to group values. In this way, they create a stronger sense of trust in each other. In the Internet's social networks, membership is also voluntary, but this affiliation becomes something as natural as a religion for many people. Membership in a small group in which members know each other personally has the function of a large family or tribe. It gives the individual a sense of belonging and identification through other people around him. Creating such networks of trust on the Internet is only possible as a spontaneous process. Local communities must start it, and technology can be only a tool for their revival. The danger is that the Internet can also serve as a pseudo-communication and division. Formal groups are created but without trust and authentic connections between them. Manipulation can be motivated by political and economic interests.

A traditional communication system is built on traditions passed down through the generations. In it, individuals have the freedom to create new communities that can coexist in peace. This system has nothing to do with the model of domination and power of the mass media. 'Manufacturing'

82 Digital media as a risk to democracy

of consent or dissent is just the remote radiation of commands to a virtual mass. The actual community of people is self-sufficient, an end in itself, no matter the form of power that governs it. The manufactured communities exist only to be ruled; they are created and regulated by the power elite. Temporary groups have typical desires and interests but do not share morality. This pseudo-communication has profound social, political, and economic effects. Every social and economic activity is carried out more by groups than by individuals, and therefore spontaneous sociability is very important. Trust is a valuable social resource, and once lost, it is difficult to recover. It is a perfect way to save time in human communication. Trust between people has real cultural and economic value and increases efficiency. Trust as a social category is a lubricant for an efficient social system. This type of trust is not something that can be manufactured or bought. It is created for generations and requires, above all, time. Investing time in community traditions means saving time in communication between people. Communication strategies and language stereotypes cannot replace real trust.

The Internet has yet to be proven an alternative space for creating natural human communities. Communities are connected in networks of trust through spontaneous and direct communication. For now, we are witnessing a reverse process of colonising virtual spaces and social networks. Communication is deliberately distorted, and communities are divided by inciting conflicts. Parties and social groups fall into hostile factions without substantial social capital and trust. It is this process that is noticed on the Internet and social networks. Virtual communities duplicate public relations from real political and social life. They are expected to support creating communities and protecting the interests of individuals in them. The reality is that the newly formed groups are divided into new and new small groups on the Internet. In them, new individuals take over leadership, and thus the social energy of the large group is lost. For the most part, virtual communities fail to create social structures with lasting trust and stability. The manufacture of dissent model on the Internet works at both macro and micro levels. The division is in force in both large societies and small groups. In this sense, the negative effects are mainly on societies' traditional communication systems in nation-states. As the problem of fake news on the Internet grows, it is logical that trust in the media is declining. Any public statement and publication shall be questioned.

In his book 'Social Capital And Civil Society,' Francis Fukuyama defines social capital as 'an instantiated informal norm that promotes cooperation between individuals.' Social capital is a prerequisite for a stable liberal democracy and plays an essential role in the economy because it accelerates communication in the social and political spheres. It develops an associative life that supports the governance of the state. Social capital is based on traditional connections and alliances, as well as unwritten rules that are known to all. It is not the child of 'manufacturing,' but years of living together and shared values. High social capital guarantees a 'radius of trust' in the circle of people, among whom cooperative norms are in effect. This circle is based on collaboration, not on personal relations. That is why it is challenging for the 'Dissent' model to create division and conflict. In progressive societies, ethical norms manage to break the shackles of kinship and nepotism. It helps to increase social capital and, therefore, economic development. The ultimate goal of society is to make individuals treat all people around morally, not only their relatives. With a lower standard of moral behavior, it is observed that social capital is focused mainly on family and friends. Any action in their name is justified, regardless of the effects on society. The Internet allows for a return to a local communication system based on family and close friend groups. In them, morality is internal and applies only to the group members. More substantial virtual groups can also gain real political power. The question is, to what extent can the lack of human intimacy and direct contact affect the longevity of these communities?

In his 1835 book 'The Democracy in America,' Alexis de Tocqueville spoke of the 'art of association' as a political function of social capital in a modern democracy. Individualism is the voice of any democracy. The result of excessive individualism is never more freedom, but instead a tyranny of the elite in the name of the great societies. The Internet promotes networked individualism and enables a tyranny of centralised power on a global scale. But at the same time, social networks help self-organisation at the local level. Local government and active local communities are essential for a high level of social capital. These 'Grassroot' communities are the basis of the term 'social capital,' which was used in 1961 by American urbanist Jane Jacobs in the book 'The daily life of great American cities.' It analyzes densely populated urban neighborhoods where social networks between people are more responsible for maintaining order and quality of life than the police and local administration. The very presence of a spontaneous and interpersonal communication system guarantees a high degree of trust and ability for self-government individuals in the community. That is social capital, and these observations of urban life can be compared to comments of virtual communities on the Internet. It is essential to note the possibilities for self-government and self-regulation of dissent and conflicts. With solid centralization of power, corruption, and poor local government work, low levels of social capital are observed. That means the self-government of local communities must be spontaneous in the future. The initiative should come from people instead of civil or non-governmental organisations. Many of them primarily protect their own or foreign interests. According to Francis Fukuyama, the external intervention of the elites and power in the local communities in any form can have the opposite effect. Excessive activity in the non-governmental sector is a politicisation of public life, which can upset the stability of society. Mass media, NGOs, and social institutions cannot replace local communities and always have an external interest. Social networks on the Internet enable local communities to self-organise and self-manage with other communities. The goal of social capital is to encourage people to work socially and govern their communities. Excessive politicisation is always an instrument of power and elites. It has no positive effect on the cohesion of society. This observation of Fukuyama is significant in connection with the debate on the role of non-governmental organisations in the development of democracy. The question is raised about their dependence on political and business elites. In some cases, specific organisations serve only as a facade of private interests and confuse the natural processes of self-organisation in local communities. This commercial intervention in free public communication can corrupt spontaneous attitudes between groups and communities. On a national scale, such systematic intervention could lead to a crisis of democracy.

Crisis of trust

External intervention and manipulative control over the lives of communities led to a 'Crisis of Confidence,' which the US President Jimmy Carter spoke of in July 1979. He delivered a speech on national television in the United States on the occasion of the oil crisis. To everyone's surprise, he focuses on the crisis of democracy and the crisis of confidence in American society:

> 'It is a crisis of confidence. It is a crisis that strikes at the very heart and soul, and spirit of our national will. We can see this crisis in the growing doubt about the meaning of our own lives and in the loss of a unity of purpose for our nation. The erosion of our confidence in the future is threatening to destroy the social and the political fabric of America.'[8]

The lack of trust in society and low social capital almost always means an economic crisis and a threat to social peace. In 1979 in the United States (after the assassinations of President Kennedy and Martin Luther King and the Vietnam War and the Watergate scandal), both an energy crisis and a crisis of confidence occurred. Then American citizens lose their trust in both democracy and government, and among themselves:

> 'We've always had a faith that the days of our children would be better than our own. Our people are losing that faith, not only in government itself but in the ability as citizens to serve as the ultimate rulers and shapers of our democracy. As a people, we know our past, and we are proud of it. Our progress has been part of the living history of America, and even the world. We always believed that we were part of a great movement of humanity itself called democracy, involved in the search for freedom, and that belief has always strengthened us in our purpose. But just as we are losing our confidence in the future, we are also beginning to close the door on our past.'

Jimmy Carter describes precisely the meaning of social capital, which has accumulated as social energy and faith in progress over the generations. That accumulated public energy can be used in times of crisis. When this capital is exhausted, through mass manipulation, lies, and propaganda, it can only be recovered through spontaneous communication. Unfortunately, this requires enough time for shared coexistence between local communities and group members. In this shared time and their relationships, they rebuild trust in each other and the institutions. Carter notes distrust of the media and institutions as part of the crisis: 'As you know, there is a growing disrespect for government and churches and schools, the news media, and other institutions. This is not a message of happiness or reassurance, but it is the truth, and it is a warning.' For Jimmy Carter, the problem of the crisis of confidence in democracy is the detachment of political and economic elites from the people and the lack of communication between them. The elites create a system of fake statements only to their advantage. The government's isolation from the general flow of life in the nation leads to inequality and loss of trust. The management system seems incapable of action and has been used by 'hundreds of well-financed and powerful special interests.' Carter concludes his speech with the choice between individualism or the path of return to the 'Common purpose and the restoration of American values.' It is interesting to note that Carter makes a highly accurate description of the manufacture of the dissent model. He describes the future as a constant conflict between private interests:

'We are at a turning point in our history. There are two paths to choose from. One is a path I've warned about tonight, the path that leads to fragmentation and self-interest. Down that road lies a mistaken idea of freedom, the right to grasp for ourselves some advantage over others. That path would be constant conflict between narrow interests ending in chaos and immobility. It is a certain route to failure.'

This 1979 warning is considered prophetic. In 2017, the crisis of confidence in American society led to a constant conflict that produced disagreement and posed a risk to democracy. The 20th-century Consent Model has been exhausted, and conflict and dissent have become the new model of the mass media, following the route of failure. Once the manufacture of dissent is a clear threat to democracy, the way remains to return to regulation, control, and censorship of online media. At this turning point in history, the issue of regulating information on the Internet is paramount, as has happened with the press, radio, and television before. There is a tendency for 'Splinternet,' also referred to as cyber-balkanization, splintering, and the dividing of the Internet. China has erected the so-called Great Firewall, and Russia has enacted the Sovereign Internet Law that allows a partition from the rest of the Internet for political reasons. Even liberal democracies discuss creating a firewall to block cybercrime, child pornography, or terrorism. In 2017, The US Federal Communication Commission (FCC) proposed the formal repeal of the net neutrality rule, which will allow ISPs (Internet service providers) to restrict or delay access to specific sources and information. It's an attempt to return to monopolism in Internet communication. The tendency to limit the sources of information and certain points of view is seen globally. The reason is the civic Cold War online or the so-called hybrid war on the Internet. Every country needs to protect its virtual territory on Internet from hostile foreign propaganda. The new Cold War online is being waged between the websites of the major Western media and the emerging foreign web channels in English, for example, Al Jazeera of Qatar, Press TV from Iran, Telesur from Latin America, and Russia Today from Russia. The bottom line is maintaining trust in the state; information must be filtered and censored in the virtual public space. Information that damages the prestige of the ruling classes is always dangerous, even for democratic regimes. The manufacture of dissent as conflict propaganda harms unity and consent in society. It applies to both sides of the hybrid war. When free citizens have access to information about the actions of the ruling elites, it produces dissent that can grow into action. In the 21st century, digital capitalism leads to a transition from a liberal to the so-called illiberal democracy. In this decorative democracy, consent is manufactured through censorship, manipulation, and propaganda.

3.3. Dissidents' dissent and cognitive infiltration

According to the American author and scientist Cass Sunstein, consent and dissent are equally critical social indicators for maintaining high social capital in democracies. The government is obliged to regulate the balance between them to maintain confidence in the democratic principles of the state. Sunstein argues a controversial view protecting the state's right to manipulate public opinion. Social control can be carried out through propaganda and censorship, but only in the name of the public interest. Sunstein's publications are a few theoretical developments that openly impose and provide a very accurate description of the manufacture of dissent model in the new conditions of mass communication on the Internet. From 2009 until 2012, Cass Sunstein was the chief administrator of the White House Office of Information and Regulatory Affairs during President Barack Obama. This position is known in the United States as 'The Information Czar.' Later Sunstein was also called 'The King of the Internet' because of his co-authorship of the report 'Liberty and Security in a Changing World,' commissioned by President Obama. There, Sunstein proposes creating a special 'Department of State Bureau of Internet and Cyberspace Affairs,' which imposes rules in limiting the information that is dangerous to the status quo in the country. Endless personal choices of citizens in a system of unlimited possibilities can lead to unhappy guidelines for both individuals and society as a whole. Citizens can decide that a change in the information system and the state is needed.

In his 2009 book 'Republic.com 2.0' Sunstein warns against 'information cocoons' and 'echo chambers' and the innumerable choices made possible by technology. What happens to democracy and free speech if people use the Internet to listen and speak only to the like-minded? What is the benefit of the Internet's unlimited choices if citizens narrowly filter the information they receive?[9] To overcome this risk to American democracy, Sunstein proposes a reversal of the media model for 'manufacturing consent' and social control. Compared to other American authors in the field of information and propaganda who worked for the government, Sunstein was the first to openly defend 'dissent' as a necessary social category. Sunstein introduced the term 'libertarian paternalism', which protects the right of private and state organisations to manipulate public opinion if they respect the free choice. He called this right to manipulate 'choice architecture.' Sunstein's idea was described in his 2008 book 'Nudge: Improving Decisions about Health, Wealth, and Happiness.'[10] A free society with a guaranteed right to disagree requires a new philosophy such as 'libertarian paternalism' which, by slightly 'nudge', limits the biases and errors that result from 'bounded rationality.' This means that part of people's behavior is regulated by irrational motives. In order to limit the dangers of actions harmful to themselves, people need a 'fatherly push' in the name of social progress. According to Sunstein, the advantage of this approach is that it aims to push and displace individuals to choices that are in their best interest. Pushing does not restrict freedom of choice, and this Libertarian paternalism is called 'soft paternalism.' It is a continuation of the ideas of Harold Laswell, Walter Lippmann, and Edward Bernays on the need for democratic propaganda, but in the conditions of the Internet. Thus, the paternalism of the educated elite becomes softer but is preserved. This soft power recognises the need and social benefits of 'dissent' as a supplement to 'consent.' The propaganda model of the media leads to social apathy in societies with 'hard' methods of total propaganda, censorship, and control of the mass media. Sunstein, therefore, argues that 'dissent' is necessary to create social capital. Dissent, but only as a speech act, and without real action. It must be encouraged and even built in the name of maintaining the status quo.

In his 2003 book 'Why Societies Need Dissent,'[11] Sunstein defends the right to disagree by talking about expressing dissent as a moral obligation for intellectuals. Silence in times of moral crisis is always the silence of the group. Dissent within the group is individual and therefore needs to be encouraged by the majority to act as a corrective of the general opinion. In groups that are encapsulated and separated from the general communication system, expressing disagreement is much more difficult. Therefore, the widespread connectivity and access to information and communication channels stimulate dissent. This is what happens with the advent of the Internet and social networks, in which everyone can freely express their dissatisfaction. According to Sunstein, the 'destruction of silence' and disagreement is an act of rebellion and is a moral obligation of all intellectuals. In 2003 Saddam Hussein's regime was overthrown, leading to revolutionary movements known as the Arab Spring or the Democratic Spring. The term was borrowed from the revolutionary waves in Europe in 1848 called the 'Spring of the Nations.' The connection between these revolutionary movements is in the development of technology and the power of the mass media. If the 'Arab Spring' became possible thanks to social networks and the Internet, the French Revolution of 1848 resulted from the rapid development of the press and cheap newspapers for the masses. A boom of cheap, advertising-supported dailies followed after Emile de Girardin began publishing La Presse in 1836. In the year of the revolution alone, more than 400 new newspapers were published. The possibility of free and cheap publication on the Internet can only be compared to the boom of the press and independent newspapers of the 19th century. In both cases, this leads to dissent and a revolutionary situation. Free communication always increases the level of disagreement because it shows all possible points of view. According to Sunstein, without checking dissent and differing opinion, people are prone to conformism. He believes that the group needs dissidents more than the dissident needs the group. Dissidents with popular opinions are valuable to the community. They show an alternative point of view and thus enrich the choice of action. Although they are always vulnerable to power, dissidents have extraordinary power. In times of social crisis, they can quickly become alternative leaders.

The exciting thing about Sunstein's thesis is that he speaks of dissidents as beneficial for the development of society and democracy. He recommended an expression or even imitation of dissent as a counter-strategy regarding the disagreement within society. Sunstein gives an example of experiments conducted by psychologist Stanley Milgram, which are aimed not at conformism and decisions of the participants but at the will of the experimenter. An ordinary person who has an assurance that he is not responsible can follow any orders. He obeys orders, even if he knows that the results cause terrible suffering to innocent people. In such cases, disagreement with authorities is a social value, regardless of the few people who express it. Relations between dissidents and the masses are particularly important when changing public opinion and producing mass dissent. In their behavior, most people follow the crowd, and so the group is created through individuals' reluctance to deviate and disagree. The only people who differ from the crowd are the future leaders who disagree with the common laws. When the morale of the situation is not entirely clear, people turn to experts, public opinion leaders, or dissidents. Sometimes people just copy the opinion or behavior of the people around them. Even if they are sure, it is not right, as Solomon Asch's 1951 experiment results show. People are aware that they are primarily required to agree with the majority. According to Sunstein, for most people, the moral authority of the law significantly exceeds the general opinion of the majority, which has no real power. The law has extraordinary symbolic power and gives a sense of security. It is something lasting over time and acts regardless of current opinion. Thus, consent is created because of the inner need and belief of the community in the justice of democracy. As long as there is trust in the democratic system and the mass media, they will continue to manufacture consent. Democracies can count on consent without coercion, and the people feel that the law respects their decisions. It is much easier to manipulate people who believe that in a democratic society, laws work for the common good. One of the main tasks of the elites is to maintain this faith by all possible means. Democracy is where propaganda, as a technique of persuasion without violence, is really at home. In a dictatorship, people know that they will be punished if they disagree. But internally, they doubt the motives of power. In a democracy, belief in the rule and fairness of the law is used for the common good. The principle of free speech prohibits the government from censoring public speech and punishing people for public dissent with public opinion. It is precisely the belief in this freedom that allows the development of methods of propaganda and manipulation. According to Sunstein, once freedom of speech is guaranteed, freedom of propaganda and manipulation for social control is also certified by law. The government has no right to restrict speech, even when it deceives and manipulates public opinion. When the government has a strong enough reason to limit speech that seeks to control people? What significant risk is sufficient to justify censorship? There is no such risk, and no censorship is allowable. Dissidents are always allowed to criticise the official policy because free speech is the foundation of democratic self-government.

Cass Sunstein openly defends the freedom of the establishment to manipulate public opinion. Instead of censorship government can use propaganda techniques to nudge the public. He notes the critical fact that in the already established communication network of the mass media, the dissent of the dissidents is distributed together with the official 'manufacture of consent.' Thus, 'dissent' becomes part of the general communication and serves to release steam. One of the leading social functions of the press is to present to readers and viewers some new topics, points of view, and opinions that express dissent. Democracy depends on the richness and variety of opinions circulating in the media. The functioning of free speech in the communication system depends primarily on whether the audience will accept and disseminate the views of dissidents. If all the official information is supportive and glorifying power, there will be a feeling of suspicion and distrust. The culture of free speech is not just the legal protection of free speech. It promotes the respectful hearing of those who do not accept conventional wisdom. Improving communication and connectivity and access to more and more information can reduce the effects of conformism and group isolation. Political extremism is often a product of group polarisation by dividing group members from the rest of society. Democracy is the state system model with the freest and most open communication system, which allows for connectivity of all parts of society. Sunstein concludes that nations are far more likely to progress if they encourage dissent, pluralism, and openness. Well-functioning societies need a wide range of points of view and elections because this protects their citizens from isolation in echo cameras in which they hear only their voices. Economic markets need a culture of open information to guarantee success for innovators. Innovation and novelty themself are a form of disagreement. Freedom of speech and freedom of dissent are the pillars of free markets.

Cognitive infiltration

These principles for freedom of dissent don't mean nonregulation. In the American mass media system, Cass Sunstein recommends strict control over the level of dissent. In 2008 along with Adrian Vermeule, he published an article called 'Conspiracy Theories.' A year later, he was appointed as the US 'Information Czar' by President Obama. In the article, Sunstein goes a step further in establishing 'freedom of dissent' to guarantee democracy. He openly called for the deliberate and organised manufacture of dissent through propaganda in the mass media. In the article, Sunstein changes his mind about absolute freedom of speech in cases where this speech seriously misleads the audience. Especially for conspiracy theories online that upset faith in government and state laws. The danger is that these theories convince the audience that the truth is hidden from them. Sunstein and Vermeule point to 'conspiracy theories' that claim that the 9/11 attacks were not carried out by Al Qaeda but by Israel or the United States. A new type of strategy must be undertaken against this danger of excessive freedom of speech on the Internet. Belief in these theories can only be undermined from within by infiltration.

> 'We suggest a distinctive tactic for breaking up the hardcore of extremists who supply conspiracy theories: cognitive infiltration of extremist groups, whereby government agents or their allies (acting either virtually or in real space, and either openly or anonymously) will undermine the crippled epistemology of those who subscribe to such theories. They do so by planting doubts about the theories and stylized facts that circulate within such groups, thereby introducing beneficial cognitive diversity.'[12]

According to Sunstein and Vermeule, rising belief in conspiracy theories can create serious risks to the state. The authors offer several types of sanctions against conspiracy theories, such as bans, financial fines, discrediting, and hiring opponents. Extremist groups' 'cognitive infiltration' is applied as a last resort. The government simply needs to eliminate risks by creating more such theories. The same amount of meaningless and naively constructed conspiracy stories will reduce their trust and impact. Cognitive infiltration may include hiring false identity agents and experts to provide information from the government. These pseudo-conspirators will create 'fake' conspiracy theories to divert attention from the 'true ones.' In practice, it is proposed to put out the bonfire of lies with the gasoline of doublespeak. Sunstein even notes that in the case of conspiracy theories, censorship can also be considered, which is otherwise against the principles of an open democratic society. This article is an official proposal to use the manufacture of dissent model as a creative social power. In this case, it is a strategy to manipulate public opinion to reduce mistrust of the state. The model works, with the real dissent of dissidents and conspirators drowning in a stream of false information. Thus, its power dissolves and loses strength, among the many such stories. This article is an open call for the manipulation of public opinion through the methods of conflict propaganda but in the name of the public good. The author of the article is a respected law expert and has been appointed to the highest state position in the field of mass communication in the United States. After Walter Lippmann and Edward Bernays, it is rare for an American media expert to be so candid. Since Cass Sunstein was appointed chief administrator of the White House Office of Information and Regulatory Affairs, this article attracted some attention from dissident media. For example, 2010 article by independent journalist Glenn Greenwald called "Obama confidant's spine-chilling proposal, Cass Sunstein wants the government to 'cognitively infiltrate' anti-government groups." In 2011, conspiracy theorist and 9/11 researcher David Ray Griffith wrote a book called 'Cognitive Infiltration: An Obama Appointee's Plan to Undermine the 9/11 Conspiracy Theory.'[13] In 2010 the model of 'Manufacture of dissent' was noted on the website 'Global Research' by the independent journalism and conspiracy theorist Michael Chossudovsky in his article 'Manufacturing Dissent: The Anti-globalization Movement is Funded by the Corporate Elites.' For Chossudovsky, modern capitalism needs only the illusion of democracy to survive. Corporate elites are interested in spreading dissent, conflict, and protest as part of the capitalist system. This dissent does not pose any threat to the established public order. The aim is no longer to suppress dissent, but on the contrary, to encourage and even organise protest movements. Economic elites support limited and controlled forms of opposition just to maintain their legitimacy. It is done to prevent the development of radical forms of protest, leading to changes in global capitalism. False protests gather the energy of discontent without pushing society and the state to the requested changes. The manufacture of dissent acts as a safety valve that protects and maintains the power of the status quo. For the process to be effective, all dissatisfied and inconsistent individuals in society must be closely monitored. According to the information gathered, various forms of protest are created orderly as a countermeasure. In this communication model of dissent, all information is systematically distorted. For Chossudovsky, the strategy of 'cognitive infiltration' is a clear manipulation and contradicts all democratic principles. One does not have to be a conspiracy theorist to predict the negative effects of such cognitive diversity on social capital in the long run. These effects will be present regardless of the motives and objectives of this manipulation and the short-term positive results. It is implausible that hiring 'government agents, acting either virtually or in real space, and either openly or anonymously, to undermine the crippled epistemology of conspiracy theories' will not be harmful to society as a whole. That was the case with the infamous Counter Intelligence Program (COINTELPRO) conducted by the US Federal Bureau of Investigation (FBI) starting from 1956 to 1971. It included a series of covert and illegal projects aimed at surveilling, infiltrating, discrediting, and disrupting domestic American political organisations. COINTELPRO agents targeted groups and individuals deemed as subversive, including feminist organisations, anti-War organisers, activists of the civil rights movement Etc. Thus, cognitive infiltration and the manufacture of dissent become only an instrument of power and have the same effect as conflict propaganda. The dissidents' dissent is a basis for the democratic process and cannot be manufactured by order.

Notes

1 Boyd-Barrett, O. (2016). *Western mainstream media and the Ukraine crisis: A study in conflict propaganda*. Abingdon, UK: Routledge.
2 Schiller, D. (2015). *Digital capitalism: Stagnation and contention*. London: Open Democracy.
3 By Paul Farhi. *One billion dollars profit? Yes, the campaign has been a gusher for CNN*. www.washingtonpost.com/lifestyle/style/one-billion-dollars-profit-yes-the-campaign-has-been-a-gusher-for-cnn/2016/10/27/1fc879e6–9c6f-11e6-9980-50913d68eacb_story.html?utm_term=.edef4064b724 (Last visited 16.06.2020).
4 The Divide Over America's Future: 1950 or 2050?. www.prri.org/research/poll-1950s-2050-divided-nations-direction-post-election/ (Last visited 16.06.2020).
5 Sara Ashley O'Brien. *Twitter, medium co-founder on the Twitter 'junk information epidemic'*. http://money.cnn.com/2017/09/14/technology/business/ev-williams-on-fake-news/index.html (Last visited 16.06.2020).
6 The fake news machine: Inside a town gearing up for 2020. CNN. http://money.cnn.com/interactive/media/the-macedonia-story/ (Last visited 16.06.2020).
7 Chomsky, N., and D. Barsamian. (2013). *Power systems: Conversations on global democratic uprisings and the new challenges to US empire*. New York: Metropolitan Books.
8 Crisis of Confidence by Jimmy Carter. (14.07.1979). https://millercenter.org/the-presidency/presidential-speeches/july-15-1979-crisis-confidence-speech (Last visited 16.06.2020).
9 Sunstein, Cass R. (2009). *Republic. com 2.0*. Princeton, NJ: Princeton University Press.
10 Thaler, R. H., and C. R. Sunstein. (2008). *Nudge: Improving decisions about health, wealth, and happiness*. New Haven, CT: Yale University Press.
11 Sunstein, C. R. (2005). *Why societies need dissent* (Vol. 9). Cambridge, MA: Harvard University Press.
12 Sunstein, C. R., and A. Vermeule. (2009). Conspiracy theories. *Journal of Political Philosophy*, 17(2), 202–227.
13 Griffin, David Ray. (2011). *Cognitive infiltration: An Obama appointee's plan to undermine the 9/11 conspiracy theory*. Northampton, MA: Interlink Books.

Reference list

3. Digital media as a risk to democracy

3.1. Digital capitalism and decorative democracy

The Divide Over America's Future: 1950 or 2050?. www.prri.org/research/poll-1950s-2050-divided-nations-direction-post-election/ (Last visited 16.06.2020).
Evgeni Morozov, Moral panic over fake news hides the real enemy—the digital giants. www.theguardian.com/commentisfree/2017/jan/08/blaming-fake-news-not-the-answer-democracy-crisis (Last visited 16.06.2020).
The fake news machine: Inside a town gearing up for 2020. CNN. http://money.cnn.com/interactive/media/the-macedonia-story/ (Last visited 16.06.2020).

Farhi, Paul. One billion dollars profit? Yes, the campaign has been a gusher for CNN. www.washingtonpost.com/lifestyle/style/one-billion-dollars-profit-yes-the-campaign-has-been-a-gusher-for-cnn/2016/10/27/1fc879e6-9c6f-11e6-9980-50913d68eacb_story.html?utm_term=.edef4064b724 (Last visited 16.06.2020).
Sara Ashley O'Brien. Twitter, medium co-founder on the Twitter 'junk information epidemic'. http://money.cnn.com/2017/09/14/technology/business/ev-williams-on-fake-news/index.html (Last visited 16.06.2020).
Schiller, D. (1999). *Digital capitalism: Networking the global market system.* Cambridge, MA: MIT Press.
Schiller, D. (2015). *Digital capitalism: Stagnation and contention.* London: Open Democracy.

3.2. Trust in democracy and dissent on the internet

Chomsky, N., & D. Barsamian (2013). *Power systems: Conversations on global democratic uprisings and the new challenges to the US empire.* New York: Metropolitan Books.
Crisis of Confidence by Jimmy Carter (July 14, 1979). https://millercenter.org/the-presidency/presidential-speeches/july-15-1979-crisis-confidence-speech (Last visited 16.06.2020).
Fukuyama, Francis (1996). *Trust: Human nature and the reconstitution of social order.* New York: Simon and Schuster.
Fukuyama, Francis (2000). Social capital and civil society. IMF Working Paper.

3.3. Dissidents' dissent and cognitive infiltration

Chossudovsky, Michel (September 20, 2010). "Manufacturing dissent": The Anti-globalization movement is funded by the Corporate Elites. *Global Research.* www.globalresearch.ca/manufacturing-dissent-the-anti-globalization-movement-is-funded-by-the-corporate-elites/21110 (Last visited 16.06.2020).
Greenwald, Glenn. (January 15, 2010). Obama confidant's spine-chilling proposal, Cass Sunstein wants the government to "cognitively infiltrate" anti-government groups. *Salon.* www.salon.com/2010/01/15/sunstein_2/ (Last visited 16.06.2020).
Griffin, David Ray (2011). *Cognitive infiltration: An Obama appointee's plan to undermine the 9/11 conspiracy theory.* Northampton, MA: Interlink Books.
Sunstein, C. R. (2005). *Why societies need dissent* (Vol. 9). Cambridge, MA: Harvard University Press.
Sunstein, C., & C. R. Sunstein (2018). *# Republic.* Princeton, NJ: Princeton University Press.
Sunstein, C. R., & A. Vermeule (2009). Conspiracy theories. *Journal of Political Philosophy,* 17(2), 202–227.
Thaler, R. H., & C. R. Sunstein (2008). *Nudge: Improving decisions about health, wealth, and happiness.* New Haven, CT: Yale University Press.
The United States (2013). President's Review Group on Intelligence and Communications Technologies, et al. Liberty and security in a changing world: Report and recommendations of the president's review group on intelligence and communications technologies. Office of the Director of National Intelligence.

4 Mass media as dissent manufacture

Peter Ayolov

4.1. The Bulgarian connection in the attack on the pope

As one of the brightest examples of global manipulation and conflicting propaganda through official Western mass media, Edward Herman and Noam Chomsky point to the case of the alleged 'Bulgarian connection' in the assassination attempt on Pope John Paul II: 'When the would-be assassin Mehmet Ali Agca shot Pope John Paul II in Rome in May 1981, this provided the basis for one of the most successful propaganda campaigns of the Cold War era.'[1] The fourth chapter of Chomsky and Herman's book, Manufacturing Consent, is called 'The KGB-Bulgarian Plot to Kill the Pope: Free-Market Disinformation as News.' The case demonstrates the connection between misinformation and false news with the official media, politics, and ruling ideology. For years, the most respected mass media outlets have charged Bulgaria with organising the assassination attempt on the pope without enough evidence. In the final, the judiciary in Italy concluded that the Bulgarian connection did not exist. This case is one of the brightest examples of the propaganda mechanism before the Internet. It is also a case of the manufacture of dissent, which still functions in online media. The propaganda model of the mass media in the 20th century allowed global public opinion to be imposed almost unilaterally and a fictional narrative to be maintained without any connection with the facts of reality. The Bulgarian connection played a role in the 20th-century Cold War and met its goal of manufacturing dissent and tension in the global audience. This unpleasant case leaves a huge stain on the image of Bulgaria, which has not been cleared to this day. The case ends with short announcements in the same media responsible for creating the 'Bulgarian connection.' The journalists involved in the creation of this media fiction do not take any responsibility: On 2 October 1991, at a Senate hearing known as The Gate Hearings, CIA chief Robert Gates and former CIA officers Melvin Goodman testified that the CIA's analysis of the Bulgarian Relationship was strongly discredited by and politicised in support of Ronald Reagan's anti-Soviet propaganda. Goodman testified that not only was there no evidence of Soviet or Bulgarian interference in the shooting but that, based on 'very good evidence from very sensitive sources—that would

DOI: 10.4324/9781003380207-5

have explained, the Soviets were not involved.' Based on the Soviet source and internal data from the Bulgarian secret services, the CIA found that a Bulgarian connection did not exist. Today one of the most serious remnants of the propaganda model of the Cold War in the Western media is the constant reminder of the threat of communism. Even in the early 21st century, according to some mass media, this ideology continues to be a serious threat to freedom and democracy. Thus, the manufacture of dissent model and division along the communist/anti-communism border still works today. The difference is that disagreement is transferred inside the national public space in Internet conditions. In the Cold War, whole national societies were pitted against each other. Today in the civil Cold War online, the nations themselves are divided into large communities with hostile ideologies:

> 'Communism as the ultimate evil has always been the specter haunting property owners, as it threatens the very root of their class position and superior status . . . This ideology helps mobilize the populace against an enemy. Because the concept is fuzzy, it can be used against anybody advocating policies that threaten property interests or support accommodation with Communist states and radicalism. It, therefore, helps fragment the left and labor movements and serves as a political-control mechanism. If the triumph of communism is the worst possible result, the support of fascism abroad is justified as a lesser evil.'[2]

In the last years of the Cold War, as in the case of the 'Bulgarian connection,' the paradigm transition of the pure ideological propaganda model into a free market business model began. The market of free news creates the need for continuous production of new stories, regardless of the degree of their truth. It is only important that they sound credible and generate lasting interest in the audience. Even when the lie is exposed and the facts show the real story, the media continue to play the propaganda model, as if lies and fiction are something completely natural and normal:

> 'What makes the Bulgarian Connection so apt an illustration of the value of a propaganda model is that there was no credible case for a Bulgarian Connection from the very beginning, and long before the Rome trial it had taken on a truly comic aspect. But the mass media played it straight to the bitter end.'[3]

The case of the 'Bulgarian connection' and the case against Sergei Antonov remains in the history of the mass media as a model for creating false news known as the Sterling–Henze–Kalb (SHK) model. It is named after Paul Henze, a longtime CIA officer and propaganda specialist, and journalists for hire Claire Sterling and Marvin Kalb. The SHK model, in which Ali Agca was an agent of Bulgaria and the Soviet Union, became the dominant frame of the Western mass media. Although the model is still used today, few official media investigate such cases. This propaganda strategy aims to form a certain public opinion or doubt. For many years there has been doubt about Bulgaria's participation in the assassination attempt on the pope. Most people in Western countries have been told that there is such participation, although it has not been proven. After the end of the Cold War, it was no longer relevant to publish documents and investigations, which show the lack of evidence against Bulgaria. According to Herman and Chomsky, the mass media's coverage of the Bulgarian connection is an example of a 'systematic media bias.' That is the bottom of dishonesty in newspaper work and an example of the propaganda model of the media. During the Cold War, all media on both sides of the Iron Curtain damaged the enemy's prestige. There is no evidence for the Bulgarian connection, but the doubt remains. On March 31, 1986, John Tagliabue published an article in the New York Times, 'The verdict of Papal plot, but without an answer.' This article is the end of the story and the final evaluation of a veteran Times journalist, specially appointed to reflect the Roman process. For Herman and Chomsky is a model illustration for a systematic deviation from the truth or Systematic Media Bias, which is characteristic of the dishonest mass media reflecting the 'Bulgarian connection.' Such mass manipulation techniques are permissible as part of the Cold War, in which the manufacture of dissent is part of national propaganda. What is the effect of such propaganda techniques by private interests within nation-states to divide people and oppose them? This new propaganda model within the countries creates a Civil Cold War of various ideologies.

The culmination of the internal doubt related to the 'Bulgarian connection' occurred after 2 March 1992. In a speech at the National Press Club in Washington, Bulgarian Prime Minister Filip Dimitrov expressed doubts[4] about Bulgaria's participation in the 1981 assassination attempt on the pope. Adviser to Filip Dimitrov at that time was Alex Alexiev, who in 1983, as an emigrant to the United States, wrote a book called 'The Kremlin and the Pope.' In the book, Alexiev points to the KGB and the Bulgarian secret services as possible organisers of the assassination attempt on John Paul II. In 1990, Bulgarian public opinion was highly polarised about communism. Doubt over the involvement of the Bulgarian secret services in the assassination attempt on the pope sparked a conflict on the communist/anti-communism border. This conflict led to a strong division in Bulgarian society. Despite the lack of evidence and the official acquittal of Sergei Antonov, the country's prestige internationally has been tarnished again. Many books, films, and publications in the Western press support the so-called Bulgarian connection. One of the first to directly blame the Bulgarian secret services was American journalist Claire Sterling's 1984 book 'The Time of the Assassins.' In 2006 the book was published in Bulgaria. Together with Ali Agca, the photos of Todor Zhivkov and Leonid Brezhnev are on the cover. On its website, the publishing house 'MaK' advertises the book, convincing readers of its truth: 'The Time of the Assassins' is a political thriller of the highest class and even more influential because it is real. These are the darkest pages in Bulgaria's new history, which their authors want to remain unread forever. This is the book about the 'Bulgarian connection.' This is the truth about the involvement of the communist secret services in the assassination attempt on Pope John Paul II.[5] At the end of May 2003, on the Bulgarian TV show 'Vsyaka Nedelya' (Every Sunday), American writer Tom Clancy said he believed in the 'Bulgarian connection.' Tom Clancy is the author of the 2002 novel 'The Red Rabbit,' in which Yuri Andropov, as head of the KGB, ordered the assassination of Pope John Paul II. Thus, a famous author of spy novels again officially launched the unconfirmed hypothesis as possible and real. On 22 June 2003, again in 'Vsyaka Nedelya,' the host Kevork Kevorkian talks to prof. Melvin Goodman was a former CIA general and an analyst at the Soviet Union Department. Goodman, who resigned over the assassination case against the pope, told the camera: 'I do not believe in the 'Bulgarian connection.' From 1981 to 1985, the CIA had very solid evidence that Bulgaria had not participated in the assassination, nor the Soviet Union. However, CIA director William Casey and his deputy, Robert Gates, ordered a report that would point to Bulgarians or the Soviets as conspirators to assassinate the pope. Despite numerous publications in the media about the lack of evidence for a 'Bulgarian connection,' doubts about Bulgaria's guilt remain. Some publications, as well as the books 'The Rise and Fall of the Bulgarian Connection,' by Edward S. Herman and Frank Brodhead from 1986 and 'To Kill the Pope: The Truth About the Assassination Against John Paul II' (Uccidete il Papa. La verità sull'attentato a Giovanni Paolo II) by Marco Ansaldo and Yasemin Taskin from 2011, accused the CIA of organising a conspiracy to slander Bulgaria and the Soviet Union. These allegations have also not been proven. Interestingly, these books have not yet been translated into Bulgarian. The book by Herman and Chomsky, 'Manufacture of consent,' has not also been translated; even a whole chapter is about the false accusations against Bulgaria. That creates perfect conditions for the manufacture of dissent inside the Bulgarian media discourse. The manufacture of dissent model is primarily a way to dramatise reality. It is part of propaganda, but it also works as a commercial model of the media. The books of Claire Sterling and Tom Clancy, in which Bulgaria is listed as the organiser of the assassination, are trendy. They sell more than the books of Edward Herman and Marco Ansaldo, which claim that Bulgaria is deliberately slandered. That again shows the danger of this marketing media model for inciting conflicts and creating a division with a commercial purpose. The Bulgarian connection is one of the most famous global manufactures of dissent cases. This false accusation has a negative impact and shows the exceptional strength of conflict propaganda for a lasting division of society.

4.2. The effect of the 'lying press' (Lügenpresse)

As a representative of the Frankfurt School in Germany, Jürgen Habermas employs critical methods toward media research. These methods search for deviations from the 'communicative mind' and the discovery of 'systematic distortions of communication.' This critical method of German theory puts the public interest above any other corporate, personal, or group interest. The effects of mass media in the public sphere of national culture must be studied. Every media survey is commissioned by a state, public, or private organisation. The question of the ethical norms and morals of the researcher is paramount in determining the goals and objectives of the study. The German model of media development (after the fall of the Berlin Wall and the unification of the German Democratic Republic and the Federal Republic of Germany) is interesting for exploring the transition from the media in the totalitarian regime to free and independent media. In practice, this transition from the 'manufacture of consent' model to a freer system in which no manufacturing is required and dissent is possible. The citizens of a united Germany must now reach an agreement on their own, in a free dialogue in the public sphere. The transition in Germany is engaging with the advent of the manufacture of dissent model in a society known for its ability to reach a consensus on all essential issues. It is in the transition between the two models of consent and dissent that the adverse effects on society in the nation-state can be seen. In the process of this transition, the unexpected consequences and 'latent dysfunction' of the communication system are outlined. This way, the 'net balance' can be analyzed to search for balance and consent. The conclusions about the changes in the mass communication system in Germany can be used to study dissent in other post-socialist countries. The problems, topics, and ideologies created by tension and division are similar. In most cases, they are a legacy of the Cold War. It turns out that, despite the collapse of communism in the USSR and the countries of Eastern Europe, large groups of people in newly created democratic societies do not fully agree with the new democratic ideology. The West versus East, the US versus Russia, and Communism versus anti-communism divisions in Eastern Europe are still in force. Eastern European countries face a balancing test between the United States, Europe, and Russia, dividing public opinion. This division is particularly interesting in Germany, in which the same processes of dissent take place, despite the traditional German pursuit of unanimity.

In his 1992 book, 'The power of the message'[6] (Die Macht der Nachricht), Henning Rohl, former editor-in-chief of Central German Broadcasting (MDR), noted the problematic transition from socialism to liberal democracy. In the German Democratic Republic, there were strict rules and norms of regulation, clear ideals, and the protection of the collective before personal interests. A total 'manufacturing consent' model does not allow for different opinions and disagreements. In the Federal Republic of Germany, the free citizens are responsible for creating and maintaining consent and unanimity. It is done through constant communication, search for understanding, and protection of personal rights. Such a transition means a change in fundamental social values. Only moral resilience can help individuals to orient themselves in the new world. In a free society, each participant is responsible for the effects of the communication process on society. In addition to the political changes, a revolution in digital communication technologies took place. According to Röll, after the unification of Germany, the 'old disease' of the Western media intensified to impose a 'personal opinion' as a public one. It is done through the threat of isolation or defamation in case of dissent. The media produce public opinion by imposing the opinions of authors and editors. Everyone speaks of personal opinion, but he allies with the herd. Journalism and the role of the media are limited to the dissemination of biased personal opinions without any commitment to the unity and consent of the community. There is a danger of the manufacture of dissent model in the clash of unscrupulous one-sided opinions and their supporters. This pattern of seeking dissent in the name of an increasing audience led to the disbelief of journalists first and then the audience. Rohl asks the question of why so many journalists have become cynics. The expression of reality only with sarcasm and ridicule and the search for bad news puts its mark. According to Röll, events are staged in the apparent world created just to maintain the status quo, although neither journalists nor audiences believe in them. 'Democracy, this is governance through discussion, is now only somewhat true. Democracy today is management by staging.' The search for conflict and bad news in the name of circulation has severe consequences for the unity of communities. The cynicism of journalists leads them to seek personal gain through manipulation and propaganda. In the book's chapter 'Censorship and Propaganda,' Röll describes American censorship on the reports of German television Tagesschau during the 1990 Iraq war.

'Never lie as much as before elections, during the war, and after hunting, Bismarck said. The experience gained during the Gulf War confirms this claim. The first victim of this war was the truth . . . The censorship of Baghdad was extremely careful . . . The reports from Baghdad are one-sided. We know that they are censored and manipulated . . . The reports had to serve propaganda.'[7]

The words of Henning Rohl from 1992 sound increasingly relevant in the age of the Internet and the connections of the mass media with the state and business. In 2014 the former editor of Frankfurter Allgemeine Zeitung (FAZ), Udo Ulfkotte publishes the book 'Journalists for Sale-How Politics, Intelligence, and Higher Finance are related to German mass media'[8] (Gekaufte Journalisten. The Politician, Geheimdienste und Hochfinanz Deutschlands Massenmedien lenken). The book was published in English in 2017 entitled 'Journalists for Hire: How the CIA buys the news.' Ulfkotte claims that he has repeatedly accepted bribes and services from the US and German intelligence agencies as a newspaper editor. His task was to write custom propaganda articles related to the European Union, the United States, and NATO. Although defined by the mainstream media as a 'conspiracy theory,' Ulfkotte 's book is one of Germany's most popular nonfiction books. According to the SPIEGEL magazine ranking, more than 120,000 copies have been sold in 18 weeks. After his death in January 2017, SPIEGEL published the article 'Man in the Wild! He is a journalist—and is despised by the media: Hardly an author is as popular with conspiracy theorists as Udo Ulfkotte.'[9] This type of book and article is increasingly discouraging the audience from trusting the official mass media in Germany. The term 'Lügenprese' (False Press), which has been popular since the 19th century and the 1948 revolution (Märzrevolution), is already being used again. It was also used by both Nazi propaganda and student unrest in 1968. The term started to be used again at the end of 2014 by the far-right political movement 'PEGIDA' (Patriotische Europäer Gegen die Islamisierung des Abendlandes). PEGIDA supporters were convinced that the official mass media do not objectively reflect the wave of refugees after the war in Syria. Particular attention was paid to the case of sexual attacks on New Year's Eve 2016 in Cologne. The word 'Lügenpresse' was chosen as 'non-word' or 'anti-word' (Unwort des Jahres) for 2014 of the Gesellschaft für Deutsche Sprache. In 2015, German President Joachim Gauck personally criticised the term 'Lügenpresse' as 'forgotten historical nonsense'[10] by the age of Nazism. However, following the incidents with immigrants in Cologne and other cities, public media such as the ZDF acknowledged that they had not covered cases quickly and objectively enough. Or to use a dysphemism they lied to, but to protect the social peace. That was a deliberate manipulation due to fears of anti-Islamic sentiments. The media then publicly apologised to German society. The deputy editor-in-chief of the show 'Heute' (Today), Elmar Thevessen, wrote on the Facebook page of the program: 'The news situation was clear enough and it was a mistake of the show Heute from 19:00 that at least does not report the incidents.'[11] This case shows the crucial importance of trust in the official media and the need for direct and open communication with the public to prevent the manufacture of dissent. In this case, even an open confession to manipulation and concealment of information attempts to restore trust in the media and consent in German society. When the official media admits their mistakes and explains their motives, it shows respect for the audience as a set of independent and thinking individuals. However, even in Germany, there is a gradual decline in confidence in the official media. People do not believe that the media is lying but in their favor. More and more people are looking for information from independent sources on the Internet.

According to a 2015 Infratest Dimap[12] study, approximately one-fifth of the Germans used the term 'Lügenpresse' concerning the German media (including newspapers, radio, and television). As many as 42% of Germans have doubts about the reliability of media information. According to a representative survey by the Allensbach Institute[13] of the same year, 39% of older Germans think there is some truth in the criticism of PEGIDA against the 'Islamization of the West.' According to them, the official press distorts the facts and conceals essential information from the reader. Another survey by weekly Die Zeit[14] found that 50% of respondents did not believe in the media coverage of the refugee crisis, and 66% did not believe in the coverage of the conflict in Ukraine. According to the ZAPP study,[15] from 2014, 'The trust in the media has fallen' (ZAPP Studie: Vertrauen in Medien ist gesunken), 63% of Germans have 'little or no confidence' in the German media's coverage of the Ukrainian conflict. The study concludes a 'Crisis of Trust' or 'Vertrauenskrise' in relations between German society and official mass media. Logically, this crisis of confidence leads to an increase in the number of German citizens who prefer independent internet media. They, for their part, are subject to less regulation and, in many cases, seek conflict and dissent in pursuit of more online traffic and profits. That is the business model of manufacture of dissent, whose basic principle is 'Angry People Click More.' Analyzing this phenomenon in the German media reveals a new paradox in public communication. It is worrying that this is happening in a country that is an example of a functioning liberal-democratic communication system. ZDF television deliberately distorted the truth about the incidents in Cologne in 2016, but only in the name of maintaining national consent. The media claims that it has concealed information in the name of the public interest, not because of its own political or commercial purposes. The paradox is that the concealment of the case revives the term 'Lügenpresse' from the dark times of National Socialism and leads to 'Vertrauenskrise.' Trust between the audience and the mass media is the responsibility of the media and state institutions that regulate their activities. However, Germany is one of the few countries where the official media admits to manipulation. This obligation is part of the code of ethics of the media, which has the task of deterring the abuse of media power. It guarantees the trust, consent, and unity of society. The traditions of German journalism and the science of communication in Germany give an excellent example for the future development of media research. The study of the media effects must be carried out in the public interest. Every study should respect national ideals and identity and national and local cultural traditions. Defining the moral ideal of 'national unity and consent' makes it possible to use a critical method to study media messages to detect deviations from them. The role of functional analysis in media research is to indicate the harmful effects of media activity.

4.3. Doublespeak and conflict propaganda

In the 2016 study by Oliver Boyd-Barrett, 'Western Mainstream Media and the Ukraine Crisis A Study in Conflict Propaganda', the term 'conflict propaganda' is introduced as a form of propaganda that no longer seeks consent within the nation-state but instead incites disagreement and divides society. This new propaganda aims to dissent as a form of social control. Conflict propaganda about the 2014 crisis in Ukraine seeks and creates an image of the enemy (in this case, Russia) to unite various social groups within certain countries. Boyd-Barrett sees Western media's presentation of the crisis as an attempt to return to the Cold War communication model. The image of the enemy is the basis for identification and an excuse to achieve the goals regardless of the means. The existential battle between capitalism against communism was a tragic intellectual simplification. This scripted conflict covered other interests. The official mass media on both sides of the Iron curtain described the horrors of socialism and capitalism as a pretext to capture Third World resources. Cold War was called the 'war on the Third World' on two fronts. The same tactic is used in the new Cold War online. The 2014 crisis in Ukraine leads to the manufacturing of dissent and polarisation of public opinion globally. Traces of conflict propaganda can be found in the language of dissent used in media. In her book 'Doublespeak in Media: The Language of Political Correctness vs. the Hate Speech,'[16] Andreana Evtimova demonstrated a study of the manufacture of dissent. The study searches for euphemisms relevant to the own actions or actions of the supported political entity. The dysphemisms that determine the attitude toward the enemy are also separated. Evtimova quoted Walter Lippmann as saying the use of public speech not only to manipulate the facts themselves, but also rather to present and color them. It is a successful way to escalate political and social conflicts. The observation that euphemisms are preferred by the speaker and describe his point of view, the dysphemisms are expressions from a foreign point of view, describing the situation we 'against' them. 'In his book 'Public Opinion,' Walter Lippmann defines the model of stereotypes as a language filter through which all facts help to support our interests, ideologies, and prejudices. Regarding the possibility of tolerance for the position of the other, Lippmann believes that a critical position is needed toward one's stereotypes and prejudices. Only then can we take a genuinely different point of view without considering it hostile. The problem is that we need an image of the enemy to create our own identity. Unlike authoritarian regimes in liberal democracies, the search for the enemy is carried out inside the country. Different groups with the status of ideological nations are in a constant war of opinions. This civil Cold War is associated with the excessive use of strong words, such as euphemisms and dysphemisms, creating moral apathy and loss of trust between individuals and societal institutions.

According to William Lutz,[17] 'Doublespeak' (by analogy with the term of manipulative political language introduced by George Orwell in his 1984 book) only pretends to want to communicate. Doublespeak interferes with communication and is designed specifically to present lies as credible. The human language can lie and cheat, deceive, and manipulate. However, communication aims to share the common truth and facilitate human communities' creation. Thus, doublespeak is a form of language that contradicts the purpose of communication. It means a deliberate and systematic distortion of communication. The result creates a distorted world model and eventually destroys the trust in the language itself. The language of lies distorts the clear thought of the listeners. Fake political language can lead to the destruction of the political system and national goals. The media aim to protect its position as a moral basis that deserves trust. In addition, the messages must attract maximum attention, even at the cost of creating tension and conflict. Examples show trends in euphemization to create positive or negative connotations. In political reality, journalists and the media are expected to take sides; otherwise, they risk losing part of the audience. The biased comments of the journalists unite the audience around some wars of opinion. An in-depth and serious publication in a moderate tone, which presents both points of view in a conflict, does not enjoy much interest and is therefore not beneficial to the media itself. The dissent model is beneficial for both the media and political parties. The division between the various groups strengthens their position as political mediators in a culture of constant conflict. Journalists are involved in political communication as biased commentators of conflicts between hostile political actors. They dramatise events to engage the audience emotionally, not always based on purely ideological beliefs but on a commercial pursuit of attracting a larger audience. Beyond propaganda, the manufacture of dissent works primarily as a commercial model of the Internet media and has serious harmful effects on the consent and unity of society.

4.4. The language of Russophilia/Russophobia

In line with the revival of the Cold War between the United States and Russia, conflict propaganda in Bulgaria has grown into a real interdiscursive media war. This a great example of the manufacture of dissent on a national scale. Almost all media and journalists in Bulgaria have taken an open position on both sides of the virtual Iron Curtain. The media war in Bulgaria was synchronised with the global conflict propaganda regarding the wars in Ukraine and Syria. Every media discourse offers its facts, arguments, sociological and media research, polls, and opinions on the Internet. Since one of the main occasions for conflict is the attitude toward Russia and the United West, it is important what is the general mood in Bulgarian society on these topics. The division in Bulgarian society is reflected in a survey from 2015, 'Gallup: Eastern Europeans, CIS Residents See Russia, U.S. as Threats.' It shows that Bulgaria is the only member of the European Union and NATO, in which 14% of people see the United States as a threat to their security. Gallup International survey from 2016, 'Four NATO Nations Would Pick Russia to Defend Them If Threatened,'[18] shows that most Bulgarians would seek military protection and an alliance with Russia in case of need. Another study from 2017 called 'Gallup: Most NATO Members in Eastern Europe See It as Protection'[19] shows that in Bulgaria, only 28% of Bulgarians believe that NATO protects them, and 20% consider the military union a threat. This sociological research reveals the lack of balance between the attitudes in Bulgarian society toward the geopolitical orientation of the state. Thus, traditional sympathies for Russia clash with sympathy for the European Union and the United States in the public sphere. These tensions are maintained through ongoing media publications amid a deepening propaganda war between the United States and Russia. In this sharp international situation in 2017, the Foundation for Humanitarian and Social Research presented the results of the first phase of the study: 'Anti-democratic propaganda in Bulgaria. Information sites and print media: 2013–2016.'[20] The research was conducted under the project 'Anti-liberal discourses and propaganda messages in the Bulgarian media: distribution and social perception' supported by America for Bulgaria Foundation. The study focuses on the discovery of the so-called pro-Russian or anti-democratic propaganda in the Bulgarian media: 'Anti-democratic propaganda in Bulgaria is a pro-Russian (there is also a very weak 'Russophobic' propaganda trend). However, Bulgarian pro-Russian propaganda should be distinguished from official Russian propaganda.' The study focuses on searching for linguistic manifestations of preferences of certain attitudes and ideologies and hostility toward others. Concerns are being expressed about the use of 'primitive propaganda language' and the creation of a common 'populist front' against the values of liberal democracy: 'We also see propaganda language as a free resource that can and is used as well scattered and unsystematic, it can be tightened in a relatively consolidated and state-controlled propaganda machine, as is the case with Russian propaganda today.' The study focuses on the dynamics of the propaganda language on the Internet through a 'diachronic frequency analysis' made with the help of the Bulgarian digital data analysis company SENSIKA. The search for keywords of 'anti-democratic' propaganda is made in order to distinguish the political position of a media, certain author, or article. A clear distinction is made between 'own' or 'foreign' in the principles described in the study: 'The emergence of the new common propaganda language shows a sharp shift on the front of political confrontations from the traditional left-right line, which has blurred, to a new confrontation on the globalisation-locality lines, cosmopolitanism-isolationism and liberal individualism-collective identities.' The study 'Anti-democratic propaganda in Bulgaria' was conducted with an open Euro-Atlantic position sponsored by the US Foundation America for Bulgaria. The apparent ideological bias is not a disadvantage for the technology and the research data, representing an undoubted contribution to Bulgarian science for mass communication. Interest in the present study is the open bias of research and the division into 'own' and 'foreign' opinions inside the Bulgarian media discourse. The ideological one-sidedness makes the study a clear example of the manufacture of dissent. This is because of the lack of another point of view and the deliberate search for conflict between Bulgaria's hostile ideological and political biases. The same coverage of the study in the media provoked negative reactions and created a tide of dissent in society. It is due to the final evaluations and sometimes ridiculous accusations of 'anti-democracy' to many popular authors and media. However, the research methods and technology are extremely innovative and valuable for future research of online dissent. The official aim of the study of 'Anti-democratic propaganda in Bulgaria' is to expose the 'conspirative grammar' of propaganda, which 'discredits' democracy. According to the study, through a simple black-and-white picture, dissent is created, pointing out the 'corrupted elites' as the culprits for the problems in the country. Pointing the pro-Russian opinions and positions in media as 'anti-democratic' presents them as something wrong and perhaps even illegal. Chapter 1, Section 4, Article 108 of the Criminal Code of the Republic of Bulgaria, defines the preaching of an anti-democratic ideology of a crime against the republic. Thus, the indication of certain media articles as anti-democratic sounds like an accusation of illegal activity. The study divides the media space into anti-democratic media, which spreads fake news, and liberal democratic media which opposes them. An ideal model of constant manufacture of dissent. The positions of the two camps are extremely polarised to certain borders, such as Russia versus West, communism versus anti-communism, liberalism versus authoritarianism, and others. According to the study, the democratic media are fighting propaganda by revealing false news. They are not part of propaganda because 'the protection of human rights and the institutions and values of liberal democracy are presumably not propaganda.' On the other hand, according to the study, the people who spread anti-democratic pro-Russian propaganda are several well-known Bulgarian journalists and publicists. The method by which these authors are defined is through the 'press clipping' of an archive of electronically accessible materials, in which keywords are sought on certain topics. The ideological points of the study are 'USA/NATO as a world hegemon-puppeteer,' 'Corrupted elites,' 'Europe/West decline,' and even the 'End of American hegemony' and 'Weakening of US political and military power.' It is not explained by what principle statements and publications can be considered anti-democratic or propaganda. Part of the keywords, which serve as empirical evidence of anti-democratic propaganda is: 'European elite,' 'European bureaucrats,' 'Brussels bureaucrats, ' Technocrats in Brussels,' 'Weakness of the European Union,' 'Disintegration of the European Union,' the 'EU failure,' 'Brussels double standards,' 'Europe's fragmentation,' the 'Decline of Europe,' 'European nihilism,' 'European helplessness,' 'American Imperialism,' 'Foreign agents,' 'Global hegemony,' 'World masters,' 'Services of foreign interests,' 'Corrupted media,' 'Corrupted analysts,' 'Corrupted politicians,' 'Corrupted intellectuals,' 'Corrupted experts,' 'Liberal clichés,' 'Liberal dogmatists,' 'Hidden funding,' 'Foreign foundations,' 'The Soros Circle.', 'Professional protesters,' 'Paid protesters,' 'Paid human rights activists,' and 'Anti-Bulgarian.' The conclusion is that certain media and authors' frequent use of these phrases shows their anti-democratic political orientation and strong pro-Russian sentiment. It is considered true that the very use of these words and phrases automatically serves as evidence of anti-democratic propaganda. This conclusion contradicts the democratic principles of freedom of speech, which enable every citizen to have his own biases and opinions. This freedom includes the possibility of freely criticising or supporting the ruling elites or the policies of the United States, Russia, or the European Union. A critical attitude to the business practices of financial elites and international corporations is also allowed in Bulgaria.

The ideological bias of this study is a typical example of the manufacture of dissent and the clash of two media discourses in the Bulgarian public space. One rejects the other as detrimental to global values, democracy, society, and the state. On one side are liberal democracy, globalisation, educated elites, corporate culture, capitalism, neoliberalism, etc. Their enemies are authoritarianism, illiberal democracy, social criticism, anti-globalism, Euroscepticism, anti-militarism, etc. At the heart of democratic theory and practice is the coexistence of all ideologies and beliefs, whether in a liberal or illiberal democratic system. Creating tensions between people is only detrimental to democratic processes. Blindly following any ideology leads to the opposite effect, which is evident in the case of the 'Anti-democratic propaganda in Bulgaria' study. This democratic 'witch hunt' has the opposite effect and gives rise to populist campaigns and extreme nationalism. Interestingly, together with the names of the Bulgarian authors, the SENSIKA algorithm includes some translated articles by foreign authors. They are also defined as part of the anti-democratic and pro-Russian propaganda in Bulgaria. Curiously among them are the names of prominent scientists, publicists, and journalists such as Jürgen Habermas, Noam Chomsky, John Pilger, Oriana Fallaci, Jeffrey Sachs, Joseph Stiglitz, and Andrei Konchalovsky. One of included 'anti-democratic articles' by Habermas is called 'Why Merkel's policy towards Greece was a mistake'[21] (Habermas: Warum Merkels Griechenland-Politik ein Fehler ist). It was published in the Süddeutsche Zeitung[22] on 22 June 2015. and translated into Bulgarian on the site 'Glasove.' May be is not a coincidence that the presumably 'anti-democratic' article is critical toward elites and journalism:

'Political elites in Europe should not hide for a long time from their constituents, but should go out on their own in alternatives that are placed before us in an incomplete monetary community. Citizens, not banks, must have the last word on fateful issues in Europe. The metamorphosis of the press in service journalism, which goes hand in hand with the political class to take care of the well-being of its clients, also contributes to the post-democratic lull of the public.'

Habermas' remark about 'service journalism' also has an impact on media research for hire. Each political pole has its media, authors, and media researchers. This polarisation of the political discussion leads to the absurd results of the study on anti-democratic propaganda in Bulgaria, which contains the name, Habermas. That shows the danger, both from extreme political bias and blind research automatism. The absurdity of the results achieved through computer algorithms shows the lack of a clear moral basis within Bulgaria's national ideals and media study traditions. The pursuit of consent and unity is a fundamental principle of the state enshrined in the constitution. Consent should be a goal for both media activities and media research authors. As Habermas notes in the article, the manufacture of dissent aims to divert attention from social inequality by dramatising events and inciting conflict. That inevitably leads to a 'post-democratic sleep of the public.' Precisely the effect of the study 'Anti-democratic propaganda in Bulgaria.' Direct accusations of anti-democratic propaganda have been made against a whole list of journalists and public figures. The study naturally provoked an angry response and a climate of dissent in the Bulgarian media discourse. While the influencers and intellectuals are fighting on the ideological front, the Bulgarian public is in 'post-democratic sleep.'

The study on 'Anti-democratic propaganda' clearly shows the linguistic borders of the division of 'ideological nations' in Bulgarian society. It is an excellent illustration of Habermas' concept of 'systematically distorted communication.' In this pseudo-communication, participants are convinced that they speak on behalf of their own beliefs. In reality, they are left to the inertia of blind automatism. In 2010, Alan Gross developed Habermas' idea in his article 'Systematically distorted communication: An impediment to social and political change.' According to Gross, in an ideological community, completely absurd and unacceptable actions can be justified by language constructions. This type of manipulation has a much stronger effect on the manipulators themselves and, in practice, forms a new social morality. This language of dissent and the indication of the enemy creates pseudo-societies or ideological nations. They carry out the slogans/commands in this language and are convinced that these are their beliefs. Interestingly, 'talent and intelligence' do not protect against self-delusion, especially if there is a personal interest and cohesion against another group. Systematically distorted communication can penetrate entire societies if driven by an ideology. If people are convinced that they are not convinced, it is easy to manipulate them. In this case, the most important thing is to persuade the persuaders. The model 'Manufacture of dissent' works on this principle in Bulgarian online media. Public opinion leaders in all warring groups are confident that they speak from a moral position in the name of the public good. They consider others to be deluded fools or paid servants of foreign propaganda. This blind ideological automatism of dissent, in favor of commercial media and political interests, is the greatest danger to national consent in Bulgaria.

Notes

1 Chomsky, N., and E. S. Herman. (1994). *Manufacturing consent: The political economy of the mass media*. London: Vintage Books.
2 Chomsky, N., and E. S. Herman. (1994). *Manufacturing consent: The political economy of the mass media*. London: Vintage Books.
3 Chomsky, N., and E. S. Herman. (1994). *Manufacturing consent: The political economy of the mass media*. London: Vintage Books.
4 Bulgarian Prime Minister Speech-Span. (2.03.1992). www.c-span.org/video/?24799-1/bulgarian-prime-minister-speech (Last visited 16.06.2021).
5 Izdatelstvo Mak. www.mak-bg.eu/book/%D0%B2%D1%80%D0%B5%D0%BC%D0%B5%D1%82%D0%BE-%D0%BD%D0%B0-%D1%83%D0%B1%D0%B8%D0%B9%D1%86%D0%B8%D1%82%D0%B5 (Last visited 16.06.2021).
6 Rohl, Henning. (1992). *Die Macht der Nachricht: hinter den Kulissen der Tagesschau*. Berlin: Ullstein Verlag.

108 Mass media as dissent manufacture

7 Rohl, Henning. (1992). *Die Macht der Nachricht: hinter den Kulissen der Tagesschau.* Berlin: Ullstein Verlag.
8 Ulfkotte, Udo. (2014). *Gekaufte Journalisten. Wie Politiker, Geheimdienste und Hochfinanz Deutschlands Massenmedien lenken.* Berlin: Ullstein Verlag.
9 Fleischhauer, Jan. (14.01.2017). *Mann im Wald. Spiegel.* www.spiegel.de/kultur/gesellschaft/udo-ulfkotte-ist-tot-der-autor-von-gekaufte-journalisten-importraet-a-1130031.html (Last visited 16.06.2021).
10 Gauck kritisiert "Lügenpresse"-Begriff als geschichtsvergessen. (22.01.2015). *ZEIT ONLINE.* www.zeit.de/politik/ausland/2015-01/gauck-pegida-luegenpresse (Last visited 16.06.2021).
11 Tensions rise in Germany over handling of mass sexual assaults in Cologne, by Kate Connolly. (7.01.2016). www.theguardian.com/world/2016/jan/06/tensions-rise-in-germany-over-handling-of-mass-sexual-assaults-in-cologne (Last visited 16.06.2021).
12 Jeder Fünfte nennt deutsche Medien "Lügenpresse." (31.10.2015). www.welt.de/politik/deutschland/article148286129/Jeder-Fuenfte-nennt-deutsche-Medien-Luegenpresse.html (Last visited 16.06.2021).
13 Mehrheit fühlt sich über Flüchtlinge einseitig informiert, von RENATE KÖCHER. (16.12.2015). www.faz.net/aktuell/politik/fluechtlingskrise/allensbach-umfrage-zu-medienberichterstattung-in-fluechtlingskrise-13967959.html?printPagedArticle=true#pageIndex_2 (Last visited 16.06.2021).
14 Wer vertraut uns noch?, Von Götz Hamann. (25.06.2015). www.zeit.de/2015/26/journalismus-medienkritik-luegenpresse-vertrauen-ukraine-krise/komplettansicht (Last visited 16.06.2021).
15 ZAPP Studie: Vertrauen in Medien ist gesunken,von Annette Leiterer. (17.12.2014). www.ndr.de/fernsehen/sendungen/zapp/ZAPP-Studie-Vertrauen-in-Medien-gesunken,medienkritik100.html (Last visited 16.06.2021).
16 Eftimova, Andreana. (2017). Dvoynstveniyat ezik v mediite. Ezikat na politicheskata korektnost vs ezika na omrazata. Prosveta [Ефтимова, Андреана(2017). Двойственият език в медиите. Езикът на политическата коректност vs езика на омразата. Просвета.]
17 Lutz, William D. (1989). *Doublespeak: From "revenue enhancement" to "terminal living": How government, business, advertisers, and others use language to deceive you.* New York: Harper & Row.
18 Bloomberg News: Four NATO Nations Would Pick Russia to Defend Them If Threatened: Poll. (17.02.2017). www.bloomberg.com/politics/articles/2017-02-17/melania-trump-s-slovenia-would-pick-russian-over-u-s-protection (Last visited 16.06.2021).
19 Gallup: Most NATO Members in Eastern Europe See It as Protection. (10.02.2017). www.gallup.com/poll/203819/nato-members-eastern-europe-protection.aspx?g_source=bulgaria+russia&g_medium=search&g_campaign=tiles (Last visited 16.06.2021).
20 Antidemokratichnata propaganda v Bulgaria. Informatsionni saytove i pechatni medii:2013–2016. (11.04.2017). *HSSFoundation.* http://hssfoundation.org/%D0%BF%D1%80%D0%B5%D0%B4%D1%81%D1%82%D0%B0%D0%B2%D1%8F%D0%BD%D0%B5-%D0%BD%D0%B0-%D0%B4%D0%B0%D0%BD%D0%BD%D0%B8/ (Last visited 16.06.2021).
21 Zashto politikata na Merkel kam Gartsia e greshka. (07.07.2015). *Glasove.* http://glasove.com/categories/interviuta/news/iurgen-habermas-zashto-politikata-na-merkel-kym-gyrciq-e-greshka (Last visited 16.06.2021).
22 Habermas: Warum Merkels Griechenland-Politik ein Fehler ist. (22.06.2015). *Süddeutsche Zeitung.* www.sueddeutsche.de/wirtschaft/europa-sand-im-getriebe-1.2532119 (Last visited 16.06.2021).

Reference list

4. Mass media as dissent manufacture

4.1. The Bulgarian connection in the attack on the pope

Bulgarian Prime Minister Speech-Span (March 2, 1992). www.c-span.org/video/?24799-1/bulgarian-prime-minister-speech (Last visited 16.06.2021).

Chomsky, N., & E. S. Herman (1994). *Manufacturing consent: The political economy of the mass media*. London: Vintage Books.

Special to the New York Times. (October 4, 1991). The gates hearings: Excerpts from questions and answers at the gates hearing. www.nytimes.com/1991/10/04/us/the-gates-hearings-excerpts-from-questions-and-answers-at-the-gates-hearing.html (Last visited 20.12.2021).

Starling, Klear (2004). *Vremeto na ubiytsite*. www.mak-bg.eu/book/%D0%B2%D1%80%D0%B5%D0%BC%D0%B5%D1%82%D0%BE-%D0%BD%D0%B0-%D1%83%D0%B1%D0%B8%D0%B9%D1%86%D0%B8%D1%82%D0%B5 (Last visited 16.06.2021).

Tagliabue, John. (March 31, 1986). The verdict of Papal plot, but without an answer. *New York Times*. www.nytimes.com/1986/03/31/world/verdict-on-papal-plot-but-no-answer.html?pagewanted=2 (Last visited 16.06.2021).

Vsyaka Nedelya. (February 8, 2016). Melvin Gudman-Taynite na CRU/ Vsyaka Nedelya; You Tube. www.vsyakanedelya.com/news/102. www.youtube.com/watch?v=przNArXQQbs (Last visited 16.06.2021).

4.2. The effects of the 'lying press' (Lügenpresse)

Fleischhauer, Jan. (January 14, 2017). Mann im Wald. Spiegel. www.spiegel.de/kultur/gesellschaft/udo-ulfkotte-ist-tot-der-autor-von-gekaufte-journalisten-im-portraet-a-1130031.html (Last visited 16.06.2021).

Gauck kritisiert "Lügenpresse"-Begriff als geschichtsvergessen. (Januar 22, 2015). ZEIT Online. www.zeit.de/politik/ausland/2015-01/gauck-pegida-luegenpresse (Last visited 16.06.2021).

Jeder Fünfte nennt deutsche Medien "Lügenpresse" (October 31, 2015). www.welt.de/politik/deutschland/article148286129/Jeder-Fuenfte-nennt-deutsche-Medien-Luegenpresse.html (Last visited 16.06.2021).

Mehrheit fühlt sich über Flüchtlinge einseitig informiert, von RENATE KÖCHER (December 16, 2015). www.faz.net/aktuell/politik/fluechtlingskrise/allensbach-umfrage-zu-medienberichterstattung-in-fluechtlingskrise-13967959.html?printPagedArticle=true#pageIndex_2 (Last visited 16.06.2021).

Rohl, Henning (1992). *Die Macht der Nachricht: hinter den Kulissen der Tagesschau*. Berlin: Ullstein Verlag.

Tensions rise in Germany over handling of mass sexual assaults in Cologne, by Kate Connolly. (January 7, 2016). www.theguardian.com/world/2016/jan/06/tensions-rise-in-germany-over-handling-of-mass-sexual-assaults-in-cologne (Last visited 16.06.2021).

Ulfkotte, Udo (2014). *Gekaufte Journalisten. Wie Politiker, Geheimdienste und Hochfinanz Deutschlands Massenmedien lenken*. Berlin: Ullstein Verlag.

Ulfkotte, Udo (2017). *Journalists for hire: How the CIA buys the news*. Oakland: Next Revelation Press.
Wer vertraut uns noch?, Von Götz Hamann (Juni 25, 2015). www.zeit.de/2015/26/journalismus-medienkritik-luegenpresse-vertrauen-ukraine-krise/komplettansicht (Last visited 16.06.2021).
ZAPP Studie: Vertrauen in Medien ist gesunken,von Annette Leiterer (December 17, 2014). www.ndr.de/fernsehen/sendungen/zapp/ZAPP-Studie-Vertrauen-in-Medien-gesunken,medienkritik100.html (Last visited 16.06.2021).

4.3. Conflict propaganda and doublespeak

Boyd-Barrett, Oliver (2016). *Western mainstream media and the ukraine crisis: A study in conflict propaganda*. Abingdon, UK: Routledge.
Eftimova, Andreana (2017). Dvoynstveniyat ezik v mediite. Ezikat na politicheskata korektnost vs ezika na omrazata. Prosveta [Ефтимова, Андреана (2017). Двойственият език в медиите. Езикът на политическата коректност vs езика на омразата. Просвета].
Lippmann, W. (1946). *Public opinion*. Brunswick, NJ: 1991 by Transaction Publishers (Originally published by the Macmillan Company in 1922).
Lutz, William D. (1989). *Doublespeak: From "revenue enhancement" to "terminal living": How government, business, advertisers, and others use language to deceive you*. New York: Harper & Row.

4.4. The language of Russophilia/Russophobia in the media

Antidemokratichnata propaganda v Bulgaria. Informatsionni saytove i pechatni medii:2013–2016 (April 11, 2017). HSSFoundation. http://hssfoundation.org/%D0%BF%D1%80%D0%B5%D0%B4%D1%81%D1%82%D0%B0%D0%B2%D1%8F%D0%BD%D0%B5-%D0%BD%D0%B0-%D0%B4%D0%B0%D0%BD%D0%BD%D0%B8/ (Last visited 16.06.2021).
Antidemokratichnata propaganda v Bulgaria. Informatsionni saytove i pechatni medii:2013–2016 (April 2017). HSSFoundation. http://hssfoundation.org/wp-content/uploads/2017/04/INDEX_Table_archive.pdf (Last visited 16.06.2021).
Bloomberg News: Four NATO Nations Would Pick Russia to Defend Them If Threatened: Poll (February 17, 2017). www.bloomberg.com/politics/articles/2017-02-17/melania-trump-s-slovenia-would-pick-russian-over-u-s-protection (Last visited 16.06.2021).
Gallup: Eastern Europeans, CIS Residents See Russia, the U.S. as Threats, by Neli Esipova and Julie Ray (April 4, 2016). www.gallup.com/poll/190415/eastern-europeans-cis-residents-russia-threats.aspx?g_source=Eastern%20Europeans&g_medium=search&g_campaign=tiles (Last visited 16.06.2021).
Gallup: Most NATO Members in Eastern Europe See It as Protection (February 10, 2017). www.gallup.com/poll/203819/nato-members-eastern-europe-protection.aspx?g_source=bulgaria+russia&g_medium=search&g_campaign=tiles (Last visited 16.06.2021).
Gross, Alan G. (2010). Systematically distorted communication: An impediment to social and political change. *Informal Logic*, 30(4).

Habermas: Warum Merkels Griechenland-Politik ein Fehler ist (Juni 22, 2015). Süddeutsche Zeitung. www.sueddeutsche.de/wirtschaft/europa-sand-im-getriebe-1.2532119 (Last visited 16.06.2021).

Zashto politikata na Merkel kam Gartsia e greshka. (June 07, 2015). *Glasove*. http://glasove.com/categories/interviuta/news/iurgen-habermas-zashto-politikata-na-merkel-kym-gyrciq-e-greshka (Last visited 16.06.2021).

Conclusion
The dissent of the governed

Peter Ayolov

1. Media hostility index

Whether the need to control others, even by using violence, is stronger than the need for equal dialogue? Even in cases where there is a dialogue, it soon becomes a dispute. Language is often a way of expressing and imposing an opinion rather than a discussion that produces consent. It is as if aggression as an animal instinct is transferred to the realm of human communication through language. Then the media diffuses these dangerous impulses globally. In his 1963 book 'On Aggression,'[1] the Austrian zoologist Conrad Lorenz defends the hypothesis that aggressive behavior is instinctive and one of the main impulses of behavior. According to Lorenz, the aggression between species has created rituals of conflict. Sometimes there is not even a physical collision, but it is ensured that the species will survive. The same is seen in the warring ideological nations in the great society of the state. They accuse each other of horrific crimes and threaten to attack but rarely do it. These rituals of aggression occur in the media space and reproduce a constant disagreement. Conrad Lorenz seeks evolutionary meaning in this aggressive instinct and believes it is part of our social nature. At one point in evolution, all dangers were contained, and the greatest threat to the lives of individuals was from other groups or tribes. The constant battles preserved the group and selected the best naturally. Only those groups and communities of the most united people survived. Since ancient times, language has been a natural part of these rituals of aggression. Language also serves as the instinct for aggression. All media and communication technologies can repeatedly enhance this instinct. Instead of seeking peace and understanding, the human language can make innate aggression global. For Lorenz, all calls to reason are ineffective. The only evolutionary chance to divert aggression out of the group is to focus on another group. Aggression toward a foreign group is a universal human trend and hence the negative stereotypes toward foreigners and members of hostile groups. A person is oriented toward social dominance, and since not everyone can be a leader in the group, intergroup conflicts and dominance serve to meet this need. Social regulation and control are ways of managing or redirecting aggression. The image of the enemy is a management tool that mobilises public energy and focuses it in one direction. This dangerous group aggression is subject to regulation in the name of social cohesion and the group's strength. Part of this regulation is in building the image of the enemy. Propaganda, the rituals of aggression, verbal battles, and propaganda precede violence. Thus, aggression is regulated by the constant manufacture of dissent, anger, and fear. Propaganda creates lasting hostile prejudices and stereotypes toward others. Fear leads to the cohesion of the community, hostility, and aggression. The enmity between groups is the primary social bond and energy at the heart of ideologies. Belief in one's doctrine means its protection and the aggressive imposition of values accepted by a community as unique and universal. This explains the religious wars and crusades of the past and the expansionary policy of international ideologies in the 20th and early 21st centuries.

Today the classic methods of conflict propaganda are also used in the manufacture of dissent through constant accusations of media manipulation between hostile countries. This is a massive problem in Europe, where the media of all countries are becoming an arena for a new Cold War. Formal propaganda and opposition between the United States and Russia are particularly strong. This constant intervention in the European public space leads to disagreement and harms European integration processes. An example of this propaganda war in Bulgaria is the study mentioned above by the Foundation for Humanitarian and Social Research: 'Anti-democratic propaganda in Bulgaria. Information sites and print media: 2013–2016.' The study searched for 'pro-Russian' propaganda with a computer algorithm of the Bulgarian company Sensika[2] which seeks and sorts keywords in media publications on the Internet. The algorithm determines the accumulation of negative or positive phrases and suggestions on a certain problematic topic. The US Foundation America for Bulgaria sponsors the study. A similar program is underway in other Eastern European countries, such as Lithuania, Latvia, Estonia, Belarus, and Romania. The StratCom Program[3] is run by the US organisation 'Center for European Policy Analysis'[4] (CEPA), based in Washington. It is a 'coalition of think tanks and organizations from across Central-East Europe and the United States working to understand better and combat the Kremlin's hostile disinformation and propaganda activities.' The slogan of this program is 'Winning the Information War: Techniques and Counter-strategies to Russian Propaganda in Central and Eastern Europe.' Another CEPA initiative is #DisinfoNet. The program brings together journalists, activists, and media analysts and uses their experience to develop an 'analytical toolkit to effectively deal with Russian disinformation at the institutional, strategic and conceptual level.' The program director is Donald N. Jensen, who has worked in information structures such as the Voice of America and Radio Free Europe since the Cold War. On the other side of the New Cold War online are Russian organizations such as 'The Russian Institute for Strategic Studies'[5] (RISS). This is a research and analytical center created by the President of the Russian Federation. The main task of

RISS is to provide information support to Russian state institutions. RISS deals with national security issues and studies relations between Russia and other countries. One of its tasks is to oppose 'the falsification of history in the post-Soviet space.' The head of RISS is Mikhail Fradkov, the head of Russian foreign intelligence from 2007 to 2016. Like the Bulgarian algorithm of Sensika, RISS is also developing its algorithm for detecting anti-Russian propaganda in Western media. The 'World Mass Media Hostility Index' is introduced. In 2014, the head of the study, Dr. Igor Nikolaichuk, collected over 70,000 media publications on the Internet related to Russia. It divides publications into negative, positive, and neutral, and the relationship between positive and negative determines the 'index of media hostility' against Russia in each country. The interesting thing in both cases with RISS and CETA is that two organisations from Russia and the United States follow the pattern of conflict propaganda from the Cold War. The difference is that they use modern algorithms to study media messages, but only to their advantage. The leaders of both organisations are involved in official state propaganda in both countries. In practice, this is an online continuation of the propaganda war between the USSR and the United States of the 20th century. The lack of impartiality in applying the principles of media research shows an organised hostility and disagreement on both sides. As in the recent past, this information war on American and Russian propaganda takes place on European territory. In the past, propaganda was divided into the national media into both sides of the Berlin Wall. Today, American and Russian propaganda operate online simultaneously in every European country. The result is dissent within countries. Given the future of the European Union, the effects of this conflicting propaganda in online media must be studied impartially.

2. Angry citizens of the internet

The manufacturing of dissent on the Internet works by provoking anger. Even if it is not a child of organised conflict propaganda, this model is imposed extremely quickly through social networks. It is based on the significant change in the effects of the new online media. The role of the audience is entirely different, and an active commentator has increasingly replaced the passive viewer. The comments below the articles become part of the content of the media and a means of profit. There are specialised comment management companies called 'Blog comment hosting services.' They create networks where commentators can benefit from their comments when they are popular and create traffic and profit for the site. The most successful of these comment management companies are Discourse (2013), Disqus (2007), Echo (2002), IntenseDebate (2007), and Livefyre (2009). Their appearance is due to the need for control and censorship of online comments. Due to numerous cases of so-called trolling or cyberbullying, many websites and blogs have stopped commenting. Harassment is usually done through threats, insults, and obscene comments. Some information sites try to impose strict control and censorship of comments. Mandatory registration and identification by users are required. This requires a great resource, and not every website can afford it. However, each article can be easily copied or shared on a social network with freedom of comment. Thus, the manufacture of dissent continues. This again brings the ball back to the media administrators, which are the only ones who can oppose these damaging processes. Avoiding conflict topics and searching for a balance between different points of view is one way. Unfortunately, Internet trends show that conflicts and anger attract more audiences than traditional journalistic ethics. Profit and online traffic become guiding principles for professional online commentators, yellow journalists, and trolls. Several studies in this area show the growing danger of moral anger on the Internet, such as 'The 'Nasty Effect:' Online Incivility and Risk Perceptions of Emerging Technologies'[6] from 2014 or 'Trolls just want to have fun'[7] from 2014. They show the sharp loss of upbringing and norms of behavior in online discussions and a sharp increase in cases of cruelty and sadism in the relationship between anonymous users. Another study called 'Anyone can become a troll: Causes of trolling behavior in online discussions'[8] from 2017 concludes that 'trolling' is inherent in all users online in certain circumstances and situations. In the future, a new type of discussion platform should be sought on the Internet to create conditions for accessible and direct communication. Many of the comments on the Internet claim to defend a moral position and point out violations of some general humane principles. This excuse gives commentators the right to express their just honest anger and condemn injustices in public. The reasons for the growth of this moral anger in the digital age have yet to be explored.

In her 2017 article 'Moral outrage in the digital age,'[9] Molly J. Crockett of Yale University examines the effects of anger in digital media. These new communication technologies are changing ways of publicly expressing moral outrage and its social consequences. Moral indignation is a powerful emotion that motivates people to condemn and punish perpetrators of crimes. It also has a dark side that is used by conflict propaganda. Outrage can exacerbate social conflicts by dehumanising others and becoming a destructive enmity. Moral outrage is caused by incentives that draw audiences' attention to violations of moral norms. In digital media, the expression of righteous indignation is exacerbated by freedom of comment. Personal opinions, unverified facts, false news, out rightened lies, or delusions can be shared there. Creating incentives for moral anger guarantees the publication's popularity, whether or not there is a violation of moral norms. In response to such incentives, the subjective experience of indignation motivates behavioral responses through hate speech. The classic strategies of military propaganda and the accusation of enemies of moral atrocities are used to justify war. According to Molly Crockett, the Internet business is fueling the fire of moral outrage, despite claims by technology companies that their products provide neutral platforms for social behavior. This is a fundamental issue in the mass communication study of the Internet and must have ethical and regulatory consequences. The hypothesis of increasing moral anger and polarisation in the Internet media is empirically verifiable and sets a serious goal for future research.

In the 2011 study 'Exploring anger in the hostile media process'[10] at the University of Florida, a link is made between deliberate deviations from the truth and facts in the media and between the anger and interest of the audiences. Most media bias and news consumption studies do not consider the possible emotional effects of publications. The study shows that anger can motivate news consumption and confirms that media addiction increases interest. This means that deliberate distortion of facts and the manufacture of dissent provide the media with a larger audience. In a 2013 study called 'Anger is more influential than joy: Sentiment correction in Weibo,'[11] a group of researchers from China confirmed that anger is the most influential feeling in the digital world. In the Chinese social network, Weibo anger spreads the fastest from user to user. Anger incites more answers and comments than other emotions such as sadness, joy, and disgust. The study concludes that anger plays an inexhaustible role in the mass spread of negative news to society. In 2017 Rui Fan from the same team published an article, 'An agent-based model for emotion contagion and competition in online social media.' He offers a model for studying the spread of anger on the Internet. Rui Fan's team finds that angry users have a higher vitality on the Internet. Anger can spread to weaker relationships, which means it can spread widely in different communities. In addition, anger will dominate the network in circumstances of negative social events due to its more significant influence. Even when the share of newly created angry messages is less than joy, the web can be overwhelmed by negative emotions. This is a warning that in some public events, anger as an emotion can lead to collective online rage. The conclusion states that network managers need to realise anger can be highly contagious and apply techniques to prevent the unreasonable spread of anger. The idea of growing moral anger on the Internet brings us back to Evgeni Morozov's article 'Moral panic over fake news eats the real enemy—the digital giants.' The danger of digital capitalism and the production of fake and click-neighborly stories seems to be becoming more real. The new media are turning into a dissent industry for anger production. Instead of the promised discussion space and a digital agora to support the development of democracy, the Internet creates angry people and polarises opinions. Angry people click more is the working business model of online media and social networks in the new digital capitalism.

Protecting national and public interests requires an understanding of this model. Blocking the manufacture of dissent in the name of profit is the first task. This requires a will for understanding and agreement, lacking both in the international community and within nation-states. One proof of the lack of action in this regard is the revelations of former Facebook employee

Frances Haugen. In an interview with 60 minutes, she claims that Facebook benefits from anger and division: 'Facebook's mission is to connect people all around the world. When you have a system that you know can be hacked with anger, it's easier to provoke people into anger. And publishers are saying, 'Oh, if I do more angry, polarizing, divisive content, I get more money.' Facebook has set up a system of incentives that are pulling people apart.'[12]

3. Second-degree cybernetics and Kayfabe

At the beginning of the 21st century, we saw a new form of what Niklas Luhmann called 'second-degree cybernetics.' The Internet media have the power to create a reality that people accept even when they know the mechanisms of its creation. We voluntarily accept the pseudo-reality of the media, although we are aware of manipulation techniques. Second-degree cybernetics is the cybernetics of the monitoring system. Even communication researchers and sociologists face a fictional image of society constructed by themselves. This is reminiscent of the delusion used in scripted TV shows that present themselves as reality formats. The term 'Kayfabe' comes from the world of professional wrestling in the United States. It is a fictional reality that all participants claim to be authentic. An important feature is that the participants have a personal interest in this manipulation. This communication strategy creates a mass delusion, but all participants profit from it. The idea of using a 'Kayfabe' in the field of mass communication research comes from a video essay on YouTube from 2018 called 'Kanye and The End of Reality.' The term 'Kayfabe' describes fictitious events and states as part of an organised pseudo-communication. 'Kayfabe' in professional wrestling is a fictional narrative that people publicly pretend to believe. The most important thing is maintaining the necessary illusion that the scripted show is a live sport. This is done as all participants claim this in public, even when the show is over. This strategy works like playing a character in real life. In it, the actors claim that everything that happens between them is true. In professional wrestling, these events are performed according to a pre-written script, but participants pretend that everything is real. It seems that viewers observe an actual sport, not a show. The spectators are participants in the mass illusion, pretending to watch a real sport. Kayfabe has nothing to do with setting up sports competitions for illegal betting. This is a voluntary and collective acceptance of manipulation. It is the fictional stories that attract viewers to professional wrestling. That is why the audience is ready to participate in the common delusion. The audience knows the truth but voluntarily prefers lies. This brings 'Kayfabe' closer to various religious and political events in which fictional stories are presented publicly as accurate, despite the audience's knowledge. The self-evident lie from 'Emperor's New Clothes' is accepted by all people, except one child. This is an abstract truth that involves community assistance. The spiral of silence is an exchange of truth favoring social cohesion. Even after pointing out the obvious fact that the king is naked, the mass of people continues to pretend to see the magnificent royal robes. In this case, the truth is what works best in the community's name. The social truth is simply accepting the facts of reality. The abstract truth is the fruit of a collective and reasonable plan and decision to accept fiction. It can be said that it is a work of fiction. This is a narrative told and taken by all members of a community. This type of truth is at the heart of mythology and religion. It unites society and creates faith and trust based on an apparent fabrication.

In modern media, fiction has a huge advantage over the truth. A study from 2018, 'The spread of true and false news online,'[13] shows that false news and rumors diffused faster and reached more people than the truth. The study argues that the degree of novelty and the emotional reactions of recipients may be responsible for the differences observed. The novelty and emotions of fictional narratives always trump truth in the media. Serious television shows that offer dramatic clashes are more interesting than dry political analysis. A politician who behaves like a showman is more successful. Politics today is like professional wrestling because it has become a pseudo-sport. At heart is the clash between the participants, even if it is scripted. The results are artificially controlled in the name of the high rating. This is the divide-and-rule model in which everyone seems to win. The only condition of 'Kayfabe' that one participant voluntarily accepts the role of the anti-hero. Every good story has its memorable villain. It is no coincidence that Donald Trump's television career began in professional wrestling. Logically, his political strategy seems to follow the 'Kayfabe' model. Before entering politics, Trump was a personal friend of CNN's boss Jeff Zucker, but during the election campaign in 2016, CNN declared war on Trump. He, for his part, accuses television of spreading false news. In an interview after the election, Jeff Zucker admits that the feud with Trump was a game and called his presenters and reporters 'actors in a drama.' After Trump won the election, CNN made a record profit for its entire history. In the final, just like in professional wrestling, both warring camps are satisfied. In the world of fun and drama, all participants win, and the audience is happy. The strangest thing is that the audience guesses the fraud and accepts it. In manipulation, a group agrees to deceive another group by publicly pretending to believe in a blatant untruth. At kayfabe, the second group tacitly agrees to be manipulated and pretends to believe in obvious falsehoods. This is not a new phenomenon and has been studied seriously over the years. For example, in art theory, Samuel Coleridge calls such voluntary behavior 'suspension of disbelief.' This type of phenomenon, called 'Big lie' (Große Lüge), has been studied as part of the propaganda strategy of Nazi Germany. Walter Lippmann talks about such a big lie as a pseudo-environment that the media creates to produce consent. According to Edward Bernays, democracy is impossible without freedom for manipulation and propaganda. Noam Chomsky commented on Lippmann's ideas and spoke critically about the 'necessary illusions' as a compromise deviation from the truth in the name of consent.

An example of such a phenomenon is the famous Vaclav Havel's anecdote of the Greengrocer. He voluntarily pretends to believe in the communist slogan on the wall of his shop. George Orwell calls this communication survival strategy a 'doublespeak.' Sometimes, this ideological pretense is made out of fear, other times for personal gain. The motives are irrelevant because this model of pseudo-communication works well and is used everywhere. Elizabeth Noelle-Neumann calls public opinion a social bond that makes people accept fabrications as truth, not to be isolated. In the theory of 'Agenda setting,' Maxwell McCombs believes that the very choice of news forms a false political reality. The pseudo-reality of news in the media is accepted by individuals, although they know the mechanisms of its creation, notes Niklas Luhmann. People not only lie but also pretend to believe the lies of others. This pretense is part of the public contract. Systematic distortion of information, staged public opinion, and pseudo-communication are terms introduced by Jürgen Habermas. The damaged speech of the mass media creates an imitation of communication, but a theater is being played out. One of the contemporary authors in the field is Cass Sunstein, who talks about the need for 'cognitive infiltration' in the media. According to him, media events can be created by order in the name of public consent. This development of abstract truth in the media reaches its peak on the Internet. The only factor for assessing the truth and quality of information is the quantity of the audience. A rating replaces public consent. Manipulation techniques attract the largest number of individuals and melt them into a mass audience. A masses of people are willing to 'suspend their disbelief' voluntarily.

The kayfabe model successfully unites large groups of people behind apparently fictional stories. This strategy for dramatising the truth is being used in more serious areas of social life than professional wrestling. After the advent of television, politics is no longer as boring as in the early 20th century. The ratings dictate the style of both the media and political parties. The link between politics and entertainment becomes direct. In television and politics, facts and fiction merge. The entertainment industry is constantly creating fictional stories about political events. They are highly fictional but are accepted as a historical reality. Biographical films about significant political figures are more convincing to the audience than volumes of historical data. Only one inscription 'based on true history' is sufficient, and each fabrication is accepted as a historical fact. One of the rules of kayfabe is Never to Break Kayfabe. The truth never must be told in public, not only from the Machiavellian princes but from the public itself. It is a culture of lies. It is not the consent of the governed, but more so silent acceptance for the sake of personal gain. It is the communication model of politics today. The truth is always presented as a choice between hostile propaganda and politically correct truth. Fake or truth, hate or love, black or white? It creates the illusion of choice of opinions and ideas. In this scripted spectacle, each participant has a role and receives dividends. On the one hand, journalists and political commentators are interested in the constant political conflict. On the other

120 Conclusion

side, professional politicians who are willing to play the role of a villain or hero in the name of more political power. The third country owns media and financial circles that support them. In this media pseudo-war, everyone who is in the spiral of the silence of kayfabe wins. The audience wins first-class entertainment, but unfortunately, the democratic process and social capital remain second. Thus, democracy gives way to television shows, and politics becomes a media function. What is the future of this model since none of the participants seems to be interested in changing it? That brings back Dennis Mcquail's ideas and the need for a new communication paradigm. The responsibility remains only on scientists and media researchers. The challenge will be to research a communication model based on self-imposed ignorance.

4. Planned obsolescence of communication

The consent of the governed is the basic principle of any government. The struggle to form public opinion and manufacture consent are for political power. Each ideology begins with speech, and people live in different narratives. Since the beginning of civilization, homo sapiens have used stories, fairy tales, and mythologies as a means of cooperation. To survive the fight against enemies, building large groups and controlling themselves are necessary. Scientific truth is not a kind of truth suitable for the masses. It is the truth of the ruling elite and the powerful. The only way to control large groups is through mythologies and ideologies. Over time, every belief system loses power, and abstract truths disintegrate. Even then, the inertia of culture keeps them alive. It doesn't matter if there is real faith in ideological dogmas. They become banal ideologies that work only as a public bond. There is no emotional connection and shared faith between people in such communities. Political doctrines are now just banal ideologies that no one sincerely believes. In this culture of lies, individuals are placed in a situation of everyone against everyone searching for privileges, power, and wealth. Civilization has given up the complex scientific reality of the world and created a false world made up of false news and abstract truths. That is a simpler media image of the world suitable for the human masses. National states are losing their monopoly on the truth because private control over the media means creating realities. New pseudo-ontologies begin to emerge in these times of decline of official truths. False news creates an emotional connection between people, which is the secret of their popularity. At the heart of the abstract truth of media, storytelling is fiction, which brings success to religions and ideologies. Daily use of social media can create new global communities that work almost as new ideological nations. For example, a 2021 study[14] shows that people who use online media have a much stronger suspicion of the benefits of vaccines against Covid-19 than people who use traditional media. In a time of the global pandemic, these results are very worrying. Moral panic about global problems lies in the real winner of these processes, which are digital corporations. The logic of the business of these corporations is to attract the maximum number of audiences, regardless of the content they distribute. They are not interested in the accuracy of the information or the effects on society. The business has extensive experience with the entertainment industry and applies it in journalism and journalism. The so-called serious information simply becomes part of the information sold as a form of entertainment. This new technology to suggest abstract truths and false news also affects developed democracies. The principle of freedom of speech, combined with internet technology and a market economy, gives great freedom to manipulate and disinformation. The problem of abstract truth in the media is a problem with the future of democracy. Can democracy exist in digital capitalism? Change can come only from digital media itself. A new information order is possible only if it serves the administrators of social networks, the digital giants of the Internet. The ruling ideas of the 21st century are the ideas of the ruling class of digital oligarchs. Digital technologies are used for more efficient use of energy. In communication, we face the problem of disinformation and misinformation. Also, there is a problem with many useless and obsolete information, like junk mail. Like many industries in late capitalism, the media as the news manufacturer suffers from 'planned obsolescence.' We can try to use the term economics for communication. Planned obsolescence of communication is a policy of producing consumer information that rapidly becomes obsolete as junk news. It so requires replacing, achieved by frequent changes in content, difficult access to sources, and the use of alternative facts. In practice, this is something like junk news. The media's message is completely obsolete as information and works as entertainment. Dramatisation of the news is more important than the value of information. The ultimate goal of media, like every other manufacturer, is to sell you more items. In the mass media's case, conspicuous consumption uses junk news. The manufacture of dissent and moral anger online serves this endless desire for novelty. 'Buy Angry. Be happy.'[15] is the new slogan from the marketing research in 2019. The study,[16] conducted by Alexander DePaoli, associate teaching professor of marketing at Northeastern, and researchers from the University of Miami and Northwestern University, showed that angry shoppers make better decisions. Getting mad makes you less likely to get distracted. Anger gives you focus on your original desire. 'Angry consumers are more goal-oriented,' focused, and in control. The conclusion is that anger makes us better customers, but not better citizens. Dissent is important in a democracy as a way to speak to power. Political anger is motivated by a strong belief in the common good. Marketing anger is just a tool manufactured to create better customers. As part of the global business model, digital media manufactures dissent and creates angry people on the Internet. This communication model of planned obsolescence is supranational and post-ideological. It works so well so far that it is doubtful it can be changed soon. A change in the paradigm of communication and critical media analysis is needed more than ever. That brings us back to the great tradition of Media criticism to which we all owe an apology. In 2017 the article 'Contrary to claims, conventions, and culture: An apologia for the Glasgow University Media Group' by Adrian Quinn was published.

> 'Since the appearance of its first book, Bad News (1976), the Glasgow University Media Group (GUMG) has made a sustained contribution to our understanding of media culture and especially to notions of objectivity and impartiality. For the last 30 years, the group has been the object of a diffuse and often gratuitous campaign of ridicule and misrepresentation. The authors of this misrepresentation first caricature the group, labeling it a band of Marxist conspiracy theorists, then blame the group for alienating journalists and retarding the cause of media research. This article argues that the GUMG still offers us useful and relevant ways of approaching media culture that has brought scholars and journalists closer together.'[17]

Similar apologia is owed to the many media honest researchers mentioned in the present book. It can be said with certainty that if a media study is sincere and aims toward the common good, its legacy will endure the flak of the Propaganda Model.

Imposing a new world information order is an old idea with no further political supporters. Since the publication of the MacBride Report in 1980, the attitude toward the idea of a fairer and more efficient communication order has not changed much. In 2020 the hope for change comes not from politicians but those responsible for the problem. The creators of social media and digital corporations. Former Facebook employee Francis Haugen is not alone in her desire to change the dangerous business model of Internet media. In November 2021, she told Members of the European Parliament that the EU's future Digital Services Act (DSA) could set global standards in transparency, oversight, and enforcement. The DSA has the potential to be a 'global gold standard' and inspire other countries to 'pursue new rules that would safeguard our democracies.' The DSA is a legislative proposal by the European Commission to modernise the e-Commerce Directive regarding illegal content, transparent advertising, and disinformation. There is a hope that changing the advertising rules online will reduce the negative effects of the 'disinformation for profit' model. The documentary film 'The Social Dilemma'[18] from 2020 deals with 'the problem over all other problems' our distorted communication ecosystem. The film features many former employees of digital corporations who openly admit their guilt for the unforeseen effects (latent dysfunctions) of what they have created. They openly call the social media business model a 'disinformation for profit' but believe that it can be stopped from within. Only the people who created this machine can bring it back to the service of society. Some of these people are Tristan Harris, former Google Design Ethicist; Tim Kendall, former Facebook executive and former president of Pinterest; Roger McNamee, an early investor at

Facebook; Jeff Seibert, a former executive at Twitter; Chamath Palihapitiya, former vice president of growth at Facebook; Shen Parker, former president of Facebook and others. One of the media researchers in the film is Rene Diresta[19] of the Stanford Internet Observatory. She sees the effects of social media as a global attack on democracy. She notes that countries, where democratic elections are held, are often targeted by online conflict propaganda. It shows a weak side of democratic systems in the Internet conditions. 'We are immersed in an evolving, ongoing conflict: an Information World War in which state actors, terrorists, and ideological extremists leverage the social infrastructure underpinning everyday life to sow discord and erode shared reality.' We all feel that something is wrong on the internet, but the question now is, what to do about it? The film The Social Dilemma begins with a quote from Sophocles: 'Nothing huge enters the lives of mortals without a curse.' The world is not prepared for the harmful effects of one of the most significant discoveries in the world of mass communication. It turns out that after all the positive aspects of the Internet, it is time to welcome its dark side. As this book clearly shows, it cannot be said that there are no warnings in the media research about such grim trends. However, most media researchers work in the interests of advertisers and propagandists, not the society they live in. They serve the newly created power of online media and digital corporations. This tendency gradually defined today's post-truth world. The mass communication theory must bear its guilt for lacking a new paradigm to meet the new century's challenges.

Hope for the revival of media research, as a constructive correction of the media, is 'The Public Service Media and Public Service Internet Manifesto.' On 1 July 2021, 'The International Association for Media and Communication Studies' (IAMCR) has approved the recently launched Manifesto. He called for the protection of public media under attack. The profit-based internet model seriously threatens democracy. The manifesto calls for internet platforms for public services as a nonprofit alternative to digital giants. Initiated by members of the IAMCR, the manifesto has been approved by more than a thousand scientists and professionals in communication. Among the first are Noam Chomsky and Jürgen Habermas, whose ideas are the basis of this book. The manifesto envisioned a different media world in 2040. A world in which the ideals of the MacBride Report on information equality, consent, and understanding seem to be reviving:

'The Internet and the media landscape are broken. The dominant commercial Internet platforms endanger democracy. They have created a communications landscape dominated by surveillance, advertising, fake news, hate speech, conspiracy theories, and algorithmic politics that tailors and personalises commercial and political content according to individual tastes and opinions. As currently organised, the Internet separates and divides instead of creating common spaces for negotiating differences and disagreements. Commercial Internet platforms have harmed citizens, users, everyday life, and society. Despite all the great opportunities the Internet has offered to society and individuals, the digital giants led by Apple, Alphabet/Google, Microsoft, Amazon, Alibaba, Facebook, and Tencent have acquired unparalleled economic, political and cultural power. However, public communication is more than business. It is a public purpose. This is why we call for action.'

Despite these steps in the right direction, the hope for the end of the manufacturing dissent model is weak. Media research has historically taught us a certain amount of pessimism about the chances of a rapid change in the pattern of mass communication. If we paraphrase the old saying: 'Reforming the media is like moving a cemetery; you can't expect help from within.' The problem of social networks and the Internet is a problem in human nature and these technologies are increasing. Before solving the issues with machines, people must face the problems of humanism. In the last part of his book, 'Civilization, A Personal View,' Kenneth Clark shared his concerns about the change of humanism with materialism. As early as 1969, he warns of the coming 'heroic materialism' and its waging chaos. The lack of self-confidence seems to kill civilization, and even the victories of science cannot help it. People can also self-destruct successfully with cynicism and disbelief, as well as bombs. Clark is worried about the lack of alternatives to materialism, which is not enough. People have changed very little for the last two thousand years and repeat the same historical mistakes with astonishing persistence. History, that's us, says Kenneth Clark, and access to information about the past is the key to self-knowledge. Human communication aims to create an information order accessible to all. The systematic distortion of communication leads to the apparent dysfunction of all human civilizations. The consequences of the manufacture of dissent on the Internet are still being investigated, but it can indeed be said that they are reversing social progress. For now, hopes for a change in the current global information model are fragile. According to Kenneth Clark, the ideas are in sight, but few people have beliefs, and the center of the new world order is still missing. Clark ends with the fact that we can look to the future before us with optimism, but not necessarily with joy. He wrote this in 1969. Chaos still pays, Mr. Clark! There's money in ordering disorder. There is no better finale for this book.

> *'Things fall apart; the center cannot hold;*
> *Mere anarchy is loose upon the world*
> *The blood-dimmed tide is loosed, and everywhere*
> *The ceremony of innocence is drowned;*
> *The best lack all conviction, while the worst*
> *Are full of passionate intensity.'*
>   *The Second Coming by William Butler Yeats*

Notes

1 Lorenz, K. (1963). *On aggression*. New York: Harcourt, Brace and World.
2 Sensika. http://sensika.com/ (Last visited 16.06.2021).

3 Center for European Policy Analysis, CEPA. https://cepa.org/disinfonet/ (Last visited 16.06.2021).
4 Center for European Policy Analysis, CEPA. https://cepa.org/winning-the-information-war/ (Last visited 16.06.2021).
5 The Russian Institute for Strategic Studies. https://en.riss.ru/about-us/ (Last visited 16.06.2021).
6 Anderson, Ashley A., et al. (2014). The "nasty effect:" Online incivility and risk perceptions of emerging technologies. *Journal of Computer-Mediated Communication*, 19(3), 373–387.
7 Buckels, Erin E., Paul D. Trapnell, and Delroy L. Paulhus. (2014). Trolls just want to have fun. *Personality and Individual Differences*, 67, 97–102.
8 Cheng, Justin, et al. (2017). Anyone can become a troll: Causes of trolling behavior in online discussions. arXiv preprint arXiv:1702.01119.
9 Crockett, M. J. (2017). Moral outrage in the digital age. *Nature Human Behavior*, 1.
10 Arpan, Laura M., and Robin L. Nabi. (2011). Exploring anger in the hostile media process: Effects on news preferences and source evaluation. *Journalism & Mass Communication Quarterly*, 88(1), 5–22.
11 Fan, Rui, et al. (2014). Anger is more influential than joy: Sentiment correlation in Weibo. *PLoS One*, 9(10), e110184.
12 Frances Haugen.CBSNews. *60 Minutes*. www.cbsnews.com/news/facebook-whistleblower-frances-haugen-60-minutes-polarizing-divisive-content/ (Last visited 16.06.2020).
13 Vosoughi, S., D. Roy, and S. Aral. (2018). The spread of true and false news online. *Science*, 359(6380), 1146–1151.
14 Examining the effect of information channel on COVID-19 vaccine acceptance. (12.05.2021). https://journals.plos.org/plosone/article?id=10.1371/journal.pone.0251095 (Last visited 16.12.2021).
15 Bracci, Aria. (15.08.2019). *Buy angry: Be happy*. Northwestern University. https://damore-mckim.northeastern.edu/news/buy-angry-be-happy/ (Last visited 16.06.2020).
16 Khan, U., A. DePaoli, and M. Maimaran. (2019). The unique role of anger among negative emotions in goal-directed decision making. *Journal of the Association for Consumer Research*, 4(1), 65–76. www.journals.uchicago.edu/doi/abs/10.1086/701028?mobileUi=0&.
17 Quinn, A. (2007). Contrary to claims, conventions and culture: An apologia for the Glasgow University Media Group. *International Journal of Media & Cultural Politics*, 3(1), 5–24.
18 The Social Dilemma. (2020). www.thesocialdilemma.com/the-dilemma/ (Last visited 16.12.2021).
19 DiResta, Renee. (27.06.2019). Media and disinformation: What's at stake for democracy? *YouTube*. www.youtube.com/watch?v=7FahDJqYCbY (Last visited 10.10.2021).

Reference list

1. Media hostility index

Antidemokratichnata propaganda v Bulgaria. Informatsionni saytove i pechatni medii:2013–2016 (April 11, 2017). HSSFoundation. http://hssfoundation.org/%D0%BF%D1%80%D0%B5%D0%B4%D1%81%D1%82%D0%B0%D0%B2%D1%8F%D0%BD%D0%B5-%D0%BD%D0%B0-%D0%B4%D0%B0%D0%BD%D0%BD%D0%B8/ (Last visited 16.06.2021).

Center for European Policy Analysis, CEPA. https://cepa.org/disinfonet/ (Last visited 16.06.2021).
Center for European Policy Analysis, CEPA. https://cepa.org/winning-the-information-war/ (Last visited 16.06.2021).
Lorenz, K. (1963). *On aggression*. New York: Harcourt, Brace, and World.
The Russian Institute for Strategic Studies. https://en.riss.ru/about-us/ (Last visited 16.06.2021).

2. Angry citizens of the Internet

Anderson, Ashley A., et al. (2014). The "nasty effect:" Online incivility and risk perceptions of emerging technologies. *Journal of Computer-Mediated Communication*, 19(3), 373–387.
Arpan, Laura M., and Robin L. Nabi (2011). Exploring anger in the hostile media process: Effects on news preferences and source evaluation. *Journalism & Mass Communication Quarterly*, 88(1), 5–22.
Buckels, Erin E., Paul D. Trapnell, & Delroy L. Paulhus (2014). Trolls just want to have fun. *Personality and Individual Differences*, 67, 97–102.
Cheng, Justin, et al. (2017). Anyone can become a troll: Causes of trolling behavior in online discussions. arXiv preprint arXiv:1702.01119.
Crockett, M. J. (2017). Moral outrage in the digital age. *Nature Human Behavior*, 1.
Evgeny Morozov (January 8, 2017). Moral panic over fake news hides the real enemy—the digital giants. *The Guardian*. www.theguardian.com/commentisfree/2017/jan/08/blaming-fake-news-not-the-answer-democracy-crisis (Last visited 16.06.2020).
Fan, Rui, et al. (2014). Anger is more influential than joy: Sentiment correlation in Weibo. *PLoS One*, 9(10), e110184.
Fan, Rui, Ke Xu, & Jichang Zhao (2017). An agent-based model for emotion contagion and competition in online social media. arXiv preprint arXiv:1706.02676.

3. Second-degree cybernetics and Kayfabe

Frances Haugen. CBSNews. "60 Minutes". www.cbsnews.com/news/facebook-whistleblower-frances-haugen-60-minutes-polarizing-divisive-content/ (Last visited 16.06.2020).
Kanye and the End of Reality (2018). *YouTube*. www.youtube.com/watch?v=LfMe0dsxk_Q (Last visited 16.06.2020).
The New York Times Magazine (April 04, 2017). CNN had a problem: Donald Trump solved it. www.nytimes.com/2017/04/04/magazine/cnn-had-a-problem-donald-trump-solved-it.html (Last visited 16.06.2020).
Vosoughi, S., D. Roy, & S. Aral (2018). The spread of true and false news online. *Science*, 359(6380), 1146–1151.

4. Planned obsolescence of communication

Ayshford, Emily (August 1, 2019). Angry consumers are more goal-oriented. *Kellogg Insight*. https://insight.kellogg.northwestern.edu/article/anger-decision-making (Last visited 16.12.2020).

Bracci, Aria (August 15, 2019). Buy angry: Be happy. Northwestern University. https://damore-mckim.northeastern.edu/news/buy-angry-be-happy/ (Last visited 16.06.2020).
Clark, Kenneth (1969). *Civilization: A personal view*. London: Penguin.
DiResta, Renee (June 27, 2019). Media and disinformation: What's at stake for democracy? *YouTube*. www.youtube.com/watch?v=7FahDJqYCbY (Last visited 10.10.2021).
Examining the effect of information channel on COVID-19 vaccine acceptance (May 12, 2021). https://journals.plos.org/plosone/article?id=10.1371/journal.pone.0251095 (Last visited 16.06.2020).
Frances Haugen to MEPs: EU digital rules can be a game-changer for the world. (August 11, 2021). European parliament. www.europarl.europa.eu/news/en/press-room/20211107IPR16801/frances-haugen-to-meps-eu-digital-rules-can-be-a-game-changer-for-the-world (Last visited 10.10.2021).
Khan, U., A. DePaoli, & M. Maimaran (2019). The unique role of anger among negative emotions in goal-directed decision making. *Journal of the Association for Consumer Research*, 4(1), 65–76. www.journals.uchicago.edu/doi/abs/10.1086/701028?mobileUi=0&(Last visited 16.12.2020).
The Public Service Media and Public Service Internet Manifesto (2021). https://iamcr.org/clearinghouse/psmimanifesto (Last visited 10.10.2021).
Quinn, A. (2007). Contrary to claims, conventions, and culture: An apologia for the Glasgow University Media Group. *International Journal of Media & Cultural Politics*, 3(1), 5–24.
The Social Dilemma (2020). www.thesocialdilemma.com/the-dilemma/ (Last visited 16.12.2021).

Index

agenda setting 61–63
angry citizens of the internet 114–117
anti-democratic propaganda 103–107
audiences, new 11–12

Bernays, Edward 34, 43–47, 51, 78–80, 87, 91, 118; *see also* democratic propaganda
Bulgaria 94–97
Burkart, Roland 11–13

capitalism *see* digital capitalism
Castells, Manuel 21–23
Chomsky, Noam 30, 34, 51–56, 79, 94–97, 106, 118, 23; *see also* propaganda model
Chossudovsky, Michael 91
Civil Cold War 1–6
cognitive infiltration 86–92
Cold War 2, 54, 57–60, 85–86, 94–98, 101–103, 113–114
communication: distorted 4, 66–72, 80, 107, 122; planned obsolescence of 120–124; *see also* mass communication
complex social system 64–65
computer-mediated communication (CMC) 22
conflict propaganda 101–103
conflicts in democracy 59
consent: engineering of 46–47; and fear 56–58; of the governed 2–3, 34, 38–39, 51, 55–59, 76–78; unwritten consent laws 50; *see also* 'manufacture of consent' model
control: of media 51; social 48–49
crisis of trust 84–86
Crockett, Molly J. 115
cybernetics 64; second-degree 65–66, 117–120

decorative democracy 75–79
democracy: anti-democratic propaganda 103–107; and cognitive infiltration 90–92; conflicts in 59; and crisis of trust 84–86; decorative 75–79; democratic propaganda 2, 34, 38, 41, 43–47, 51, 57, 78, 87; and digital capitalism 75–76; dissent in 79–86; and dissidents 86–89; empty shell of 22–23; properly functioning 52; pseudo-environment of 40–41; and public opinion 42–43; and social capital 79–84; trust in 79–86
democratic propaganda 2, 34; and digital media 78, 87; and dissent 38, 41, 43–47, 51, 57
digital capitalism 75–79
digital media: and cognitive infiltration 90–92; and crisis of trust 84–86; and decorative democracy 77–79; and digital capitalism 75–76; and dissidents' dissent 86–89; and social capital 79–84
disintermediation 15
dissent: and agenda setting 61–63; and angry citizens of the internet 114–117; and cognitive infiltration 86–92; definition 1; in democracy 79–86; and democratic propaganda 43–47; and distorted communication 66–72; and the end of history 56–61; governing with 55–56; and manufacture of consent 38–43; and media hostility index 112–114; and planned obsolescence of communication 120–124; and the propaganda model 51–56; and pseudo news 63–66; rise of 14–23; and second-degree cybernetics

117–120; and the spiral of silence 47–50; *see also* dissent manufacture
dissent manufacture: and the Bulgarian connection in the attack on the pope 94–97; doublespeak and conflict propaganda 101–103; and the effect of the 'lying press' 97–101; and the language of Russophilia/Russophobia 103–107
dissidents 86–92
distorted communication 4, 66–72, 80, 107, 122
doublespeak 101–103
dysfunctions: of mass media 31–33; in the propaganda model 30–35
dystopia 24–30

end of history 35, 56–61
engineering of consent 46–47

fear 54, 113; and consent 56–58; of isolation 34, 47, 49
Fukuyama, Francis 35, 56–61, 72, 81–84; *see also* end of history
function: of mass media 44; properly functioning democracy 52

Glasgow University Media Group (GUMG) 5–6, 122
governed, consent of the 2–3, 34, 38–39, 51, 55–59, 76–78; and angry citizens of the internet 114–117; and media hostility index 112–114; and planned obsolescence of communication 120–124; and second-degree cybernetics 117–120
governing with dissent 55–56

Habermas, Jürgen 4, 31, 35, 66–72, 97, 106–107, 119, 123; *see also* distorted communication
Herman, Edward 30, 34, 51–56, 94–97; *see also* propaganda model
history, end of 35, 56–61
hostility, media *see* media hostility index

ideal complex social system 64–65
illusions, necessary 54–55, 118
inequality 5–6, 42–43, 79–80; information inequality 21–27
infiltration, cognitive 86–92
information inequality 24–26
international public opinion 26–28

Internet: angry citizens of 114–117; future of 19–20; and media ecology 17–19
Internet of Things (IoT) 20

kayfabe model 117–120

language: of power 69–71; of Russophilia/Russophobia 103–107
law 16–18, 30, 39, 48–49, 88–91; unwritten consent laws 50
Lippmann, Walter 3, 17, 30, 33–34, 102, 118; digital media 78–80, 87, 91; and dissent 38–43, 46, 51–52, 61–63; *see also* 'manufacture of consent' model
Lügenpresse 97–101
Luhmann, Niklas 63–66, 117, 119; *see also* pseudo news
lying press 97–101

MacBride Report 24–30, 122–123
management, self-monitoring 63–64
manufacture: definition 1; *see also* dissent manufacture; 'manufacture of consent' model
'manufacture of consent' model 3–4, 30, 38–46, 50–51, 57–59, 63–68; and digital media 78–80, 89; and dissent manufacture 97–98
mass communication: agenda setting 61–63; democratic propaganda 43–47; distorted communication 66–72; and dysfunctions in the propaganda model 30–35; the end of history 56–61; manufacture of consent 38–43; the need for a new paradigm 7–14; and the New World Information Order 24–30; the propaganda model 51–56; pseudo news 63–66; and the rise of dissent in the network society 14–23; the spiral of silence 47–50
masses, the *see* virtual masses
mass media: and the Bulgarian connection in the attack on the pope 94–97; doublespeak and conflict propaganda 101–103; and the effect of the 'lying press' 97–101; functions of 44; and the language of Russophilia/Russophobia 103–107; latent dysfunction of 31–33; manufacture of consent in 41–42
McCombs, Maxwell 61–63, 119; *see also* agenda setting

Index

McLuhan, Marshall 16, 18–21
Mcquail, Dennis 7–10, 14, 38, 120
media, digital *see* digital media
media control 10, 51
media ecology 17–19
media hostility index 112–114
mediocratia 15–17
moral outrage 115–116
Murdochisation 28–30

necessary illusions 54–55, 118
network society: reality of 21–22; rise of dissent in 14–23
new media 4, 10–12, 15–18, 22, 38, 54, 76, 116
New World Information Order 3, 17–18, 23–30, 122
Noelle-Neumann, Elizabeth 34, 47–50, 63, 119; *see also* spiral of silence
normality *see* pseudonormality

obsolescence, planned 120–124
online media model, Propaganda 2.0 33–35

planned obsolescence 120–124
Pope John Paul II 94–97
power: language of 69–71; of the powerless 59–61
propaganda: conflict propaganda 101–103; need for democratic propaganda 44–45; *see also* propaganda model
propaganda model 51–57, 72, 78, 80, 87, 94–96, 122; dysfunctions in 30–35; in the 21st century 52–54
Propaganda 2.0 5, 33–35, 53, 56
pseudo-communication 4, 15, 62, 76, 81–82, 107, 117–119; of the virtual masses 68–69
pseudo-environment 40–43, 54, 118
pseudo news 63–66
pseudonormality 68, 71–72
public opinion 26–28; and democratic propaganda 43–44; end of 49; and the risk to democracy 42–43; as a social bond 48; staging 67–68; why manipulate public opinion 45–46
public relations 38, 62, 67, 82; and democratic propaganda 43–44

'Public Service Media and Public Service Internet Manifesto, The' 123

research, new 10–11, 13–14
risk to democracy: and cognitive infiltration 90–92; and crisis of trust 84–86; and decorative democracy 77–79; and digital capitalism 75–76; and dissidents' dissent 86–89; and public opinion 42–43; and social capital 79–84; *see also* democracy
Russophilia/Russophobia 103–107

second-degree cybernetics 65–66, 117–120
self-monitoring management 63–64
Semantic Web 15, 20
social bond 47, 113, 119; public opinion as 48
social capital 79–84
social control 35, 44, 48–49, 51, 86, 89
'Social Dilemma, The' 122–123
social order 14, 45, 80
social system 9, 63, 68, 82; ideal complex social system 64–65
Soviets 27, 94–95, 97, 114
spiral of silence 34, 47–50, 117–118
Sunstein, Cass 86–91, 119

theory of mass communication: agenda setting 61–63; democratic propaganda 43–47; distorted communication 66–72; the end of history 56–61; manufacture of consent 38–43; the propaganda model 51–56; pseudo news 63–66; the spiral of silence 47–50; *see also* mass communication
trust: crisis of 84–86; in democracy 79–86

UNESCO 23–28; *see also* New World Information Order
unwritten consent laws 50

virtual masses 55; pseudo-communication of 68–69

Web 2.0 14–15

Zero Theorem, The 1

Printed in the United States
by Baker & Taylor Publisher Services